Beverley

TOWN TRAIL
REVISITED

With best wishes

By Peter Lee and Peter Hick
with help from Pamela Hopkins and Berna Moody

Peter Hick

Pam Hopkins

Berna Moody.

Printed in Yorkshire by Hart and Clough Ltd.

NAB WOOD PUBLICATIONS
1 Pasture Lane, Beverley, HU17 8DU
United Kingdom.

ISBN: 978-1-9162300-2-6

Front cover:	Yellow Boots. PL/Hart and Clough
Back cover:	Hart and Clough
Pages iv/v:	Map of Beverley Town Trail courtesy of Pamela Hopkins and Berna Moody

Beverley Town Ce[ntre]

Map Labels

NORTH BAR WITHOUT
WYLIES ROAD
NORTH BAR
NORTH BAR WITHIN
A1035 YORK ROAD
TIGER LANE
VICAR LANE
WALTHAM LANE
ST MARY'S CHURCH
HENGATE
LADYGATE
SOW HILL
BUS STATION
NORWOOD A1035
MORTON LANE
NEW WALKERGATE ROAD
SATURDAY MARKET
MARKET CROSS
DOG & DUCK LN
SWABY'S YARD
SPENCER STREET
WALKERGATE
SCHOOL LANE
DYER LANE
SATURDAY MARKET
BUTCHER ROW
CROSS BRIDGE
WEDNESDAY MARKET
WILBERT LANE
WILBERT GA[RTH]
RAILW[AY]
TOLL GAVEL
LAIRGATE
LANDRESS LANE
GUILDHALL
REGISTER SQ
WELL LANE
CROSS STREET
LORD ROBERTS RD
PRINCES GARDENS
REGENT STREET
HIGHGATE
ST JOHN STREET
COUNTY HALL
CHAMPNEYS ROAD
TREASURE HOUSE
LIBRARY & ART GALLERIES
MINSTER MOORGATE
LAIRGATE
ADMIRAL WALKER ROAD
A164
KELDGATE
MIN[STER]
0   ½ kilometre

KEY

WALK 1
6 CARTMEN
7 GLOVERS
8 JERKIN MAKERS
9 MINSTRELS
10 ARMOURERS
11 BRICKLAYERS
12 FARRIERS & LORIMERS (BLACKSMITHS)
13 WIND MILLERS
14 BAKERS
15 GOLDSMITHS
16 HATTERS
17 FLETCHERS

WALK 2
1 BUTCHERS
2 WALKERS
3 CORDWAINERS
4 SPINNERS
5 DYERS
18 TAILORS
19 APOTHECARIES
20 BARBER SURGEONS
21 MERCHANTS
22 FISH TRADERS

WALK 3
23 PRINTERS
24 MASONS
25 BREWERS
26 CARPENTERS
36 SCRIVENERS
37 LOCKSMITHS
38 CANDLE MAKERS
39 FISHMONGERS

WALK 4
27 SADDLERS
28 WEAVERS
29 ROPE MAKERS
30 CREELERS
31 WILDFOWLERS
32 POTTERS
33 WATER MILLERS
34 TANNERS
35 COOPERS
40 COOKS

granny
classed as
wooanronsy!!
No posh lamps

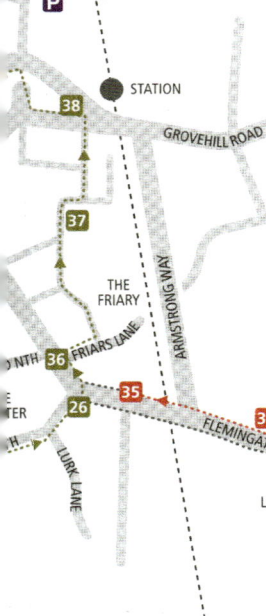

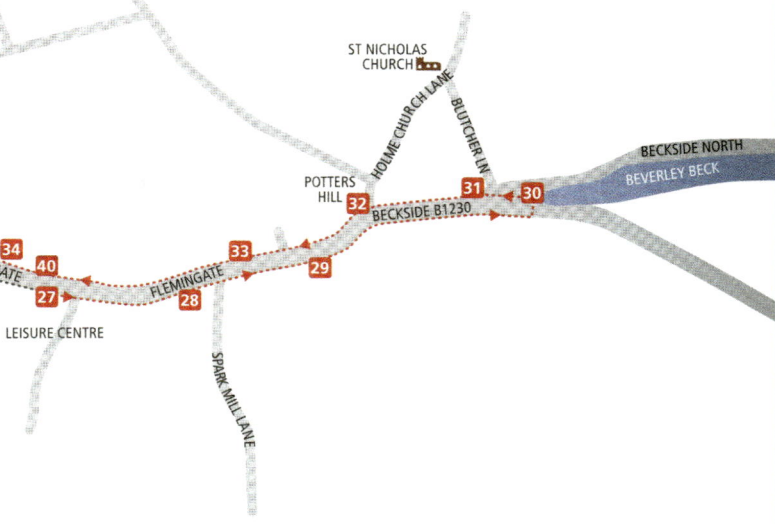

TO YORK

A1079
A614

TO DRIFFIELD   TO BRIDLINGTON
A164

A1079

A1034

BEVERLEY

A1034

TO LEEDS
MANCHESTER

M62

A164

A63

KINGSTON
UPON HULL

HUMBER
BRIDGE

A15
TO LINCOLN

HULL – SCARBOROUGH LINE

TRINITY LANE

P

STATION

GROVEHILL ROAD

38

37

THE
FRIARY

FRIARS LANE

ARMSTRONG WAY

36 NTH

TER

36

26

35

40

34

27

28

FLEMINGATE

FLEMINGATE

LEISURE CENTRE

LURK LANE

SPARK MILL LANE

ST NICHOLAS
CHURCH

HOLME CHURCH LANE

BUTCHER LN

POTTERS
HILL

32

33

29

31

30

BECKSIDE B1230

BECKSIDE NORTH

BEVERLEY BECK

½ mile

CONTENTS

Numbers in brackets refer to the Art Installation numbers on map

HELP ⋀ for Health

Helping East Yorkshire & Lincolnshire People

All profits from the sale of this book
will be given to Help For Health
who celebrate their 20th anniversary in 2022

ABOUT THIS BOOK

The Beverley Town Trail consists of 40 art installations symbolising the Town Guilds which were such an important part of the thriving commerce of Beverley in the Middle Ages. The art forms vary from engravings on paving stones, to hanging effigies, to small and large sculptures - each one different in context and design. They are laid out in four walks around the winding streets of our historic town. The concept of The Trail is to provide a stimulating and educational journey through Beverley for both young and old, with the added bonus and fun of discovering the installations -not always easy but well worth the effort.

The original Town Trail guide, written by Pamela Hopkins and Berna Moody, sets the scene in some detail. In this book we have sought to bring a different slant to the art forms by depicting them in paintings (some quirky, some not), each paired with a poem by Peter Hick and a little added writing to promote interest and knowledge. We hope you will enjoy the book. All profits will go to the local charity Help for Health which will be celebrating their 20th Anniversary in 2022 - twenty years of providing financial support for medically related projects in Hull, East Yorkshire and North Lincolnshire.

HOW TO USE THIS BOOK

There are several different ways in which you may choose to use this book; integral to all are the four separate maps showing the sites of the art installations.

The narrative starts quite deliberately with the Merchants art form in Walk Two, found very near to the Treasure House - because the writings here will tell you about the Town Guilds, the central theme of the book. In addition, you may well have just purchased the book in the Treasure House, so you will only need to walk down Champney Road to begin!!

Ideally, you may have had chance to glance through the pages, look at the maps, then plan your walk through Beverley, search out the art forms and then read out the poems and writings as you look at them. The book has been kept to a handy size so you can carry it with you. We recommend you combine our book with Pamela's and Berna's original guide.*

Each walk will take about 90 minutes to two hours, not because they are a long walk but because the fun of finding the installations can be time consuming. From personal experience there is nothing worse than not being able to find the art form - especially when the short attention span of young children is factored in. Later on we have provided a quick guide to the exact locations - only to be used if you are in difficulty!!

On the other hand it may suit you to start with a different 'Walk' first - this is no problem, you can choose which ever suits your location and time available.

Alternatively, particularly if you are already familiar with Beverley and The Town Trail, you may choose to sit in the comfort of your own home and just read the book and absorb the atmosphere of medieval Beverley.

* The Beverley Town Trail by Pamela Hopkins and Berna Moody, available from the Tourist Information Centre, The Treasure House, Champney Road, Beverley HU17 8HE.

PROLOGUE

Trail Blaze by Tom Lee

The origin of your trail
is wherever you choose to start.

A deep-rooted sense of place may
anchor you to the Westwood.

A spiritual journey may start at St Mary`s and
end at The Minster.

The Marketplace may be where you bought your first record,
took a date to the cinema or had fish and chips up Toll Gavel.

Is this a rainy-day activity?
Or is your trail solar-powered
by the sun, glinting off the Market Cross?

Courtesy of Katy Marriott.

NEW WALKER GATE

SPENCER St.

SCHOOL LANE

WALKER

THE TOWN TRAIL

WALK TWO

SWABY'S YARD

DYER LANE

DOG + DUCK LANE

MADDER

LADYGATE

SATURDAY MARKET

LAIRGATE

3

4

5

19

13

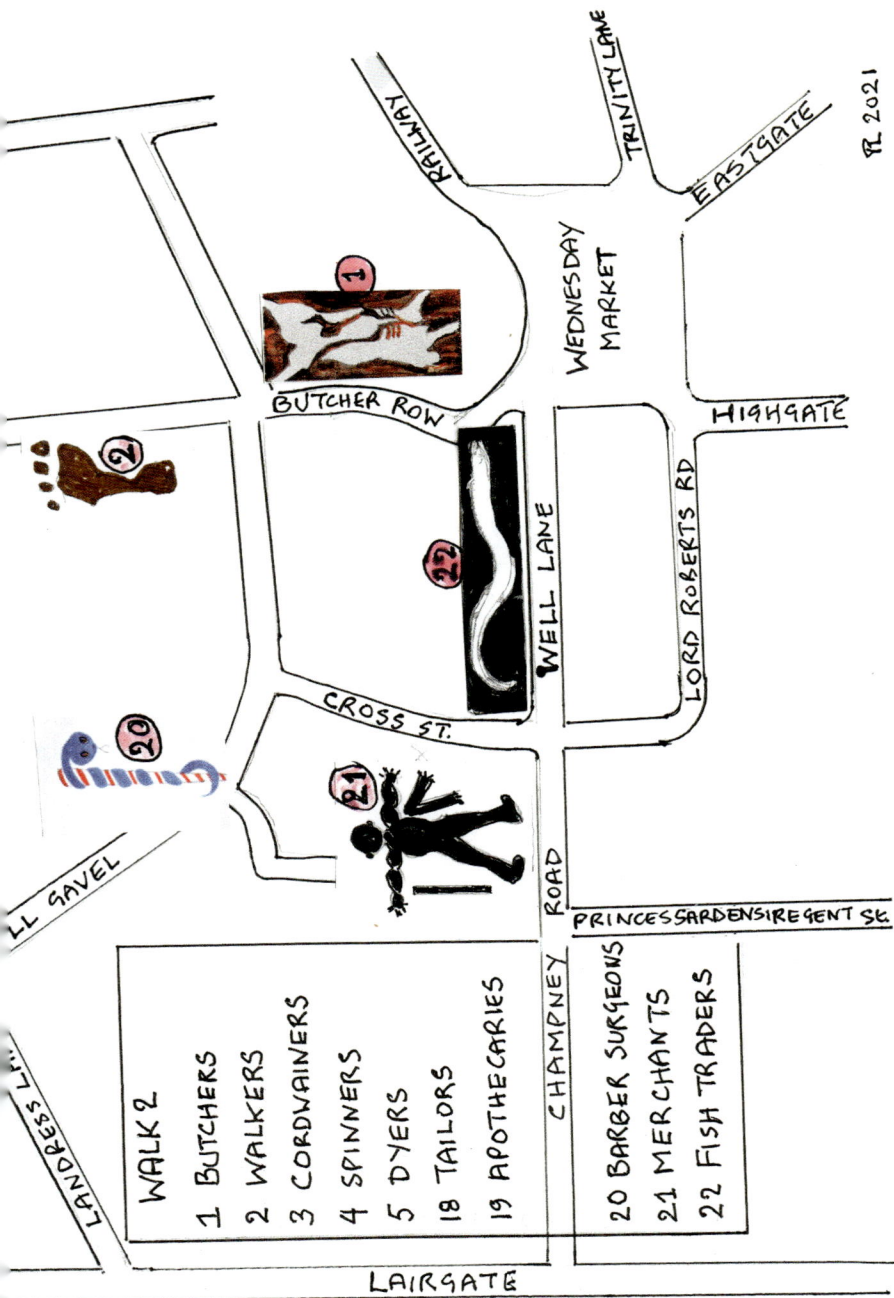

RAILWAY

TRINITY LANE

EASTGATE

R 2021

WEDNESDAY MARKET

①

BUTCHER ROW

HIGHGATE

②

22

WELL LANE

LORD ROBERTS RD

CROSS ST.

20

21

LL GAVEL

CHAMPNEY ROAD

PRINCESS ARDENS IRE REGENT SE

WALK 2

1 BUTCHERS
2 WALKERS
3 CORDWAINERS
4 SPINNERS
5 DYERS
18 TAILORS
19 APOTHECARIES

20 BARBER SURGEONS
21 MERCHANTS
22 FISH TRADERS

LANDRESS LN

LAIRGATE

3

GUILDS – MERCHANTS
and CRAFTMENS GUILDS

Guild or gild comes from the Saxon word *gilden* meaning to pay or yield, because members of a guild were expected to contribute to the finances, i.e. pay a membership fee - just like a golf club or sports club today! In the Middle Ages there were two types of guild – The Merchants who were traders or merchants and controlled trade in the town, and the Craftsmen who were the artisans and craftsmen.

Both the groups of guilds had similar purposes:

> to regulate membership

> to restrict competition

> to regulate prices of goods

> to regulate quality control

> to relate with local government (mainly Merchants)

> to provide employment and training for workers (mainly Craftsmen)

> to provide aid for guild members if ill or in financial difficulty

> to encourage religion

The Merchants were the 'big boys' in town and the wealthiest too. They were able to control trade in their own town and internationally as well. They often did deals with 'The Crown' - they bought charters which enabled them to avoid feudal taxes and set their own taxes for the local craftsmen. The top of the hierarchy were the Masters who were often involved with and held influential positions in local government. The Masters alone decided when a member should be elevated to 'Master'.

The Craftsmens' Guilds were founded for nearly all the local artisans and craftsmen, many of whom feature in this book. Aside from making and selling goods they provided employment and training. The trainees entered as paid apprentices (often as young as twelve years old), progressed to journeymen and, after five years, provided they could prove their skills, could be made a Master and set up their own business. It was possible for a Craftsmen's Master to become a member of the Merchant Guild - which might enable him to make more money by selling his goods further afield and improve his 'social' standing.

In Beverley the twelve governors of the town, who were mainly members of the Merchants' Guild, appointed two searchers from each guild who would check on the quality and price of the goods being made by the craftsmen, and make sure appropriate taxes were being paid – hence, I presume, the presence of the weights and measures shown on 'The Merchant Man' exhibit.

The Syndics of the Drapers Guild Rembrandt 1662
Courtesy Wiki Commons

INCH · FOOT · YARD · ROD · POLE · PERCH

THE MERCHANTS

In an odd little square off Cross Street Road
Is an interesting exhibit to the Merchants of old -
On a stainless steel table lies a stainless steel man
With four arms and two legs, what it means
I'll be damned.

But look closely and you'll see round the edge
The weights and measures The Guild used to check
On the goods which were bought by the Beverley men
And charged by the Merchants for the service, you ken
I'll be damned.

There's inches and feet, rod, pole and perch,
A yardstick on top, and with a bit of a search
There's chain, furlong, mile and even a league,
Though what some mean will cause some intrigue
I'll be damned.

On the side at the top there's a peck and a bushel
And, on the next edge, there's a pound and a stone;
And last in the line is a hundred weight...groan...
Which I'm sure the boys did when they paid up their loan
I'll be damned.

Of all the exhibits I find this the oddest -
That's just how I feel, but to be honest
I think that the sculptor was out to provoke us
So the painting, in turn, is a bit jokus pokus
I'll be damned.

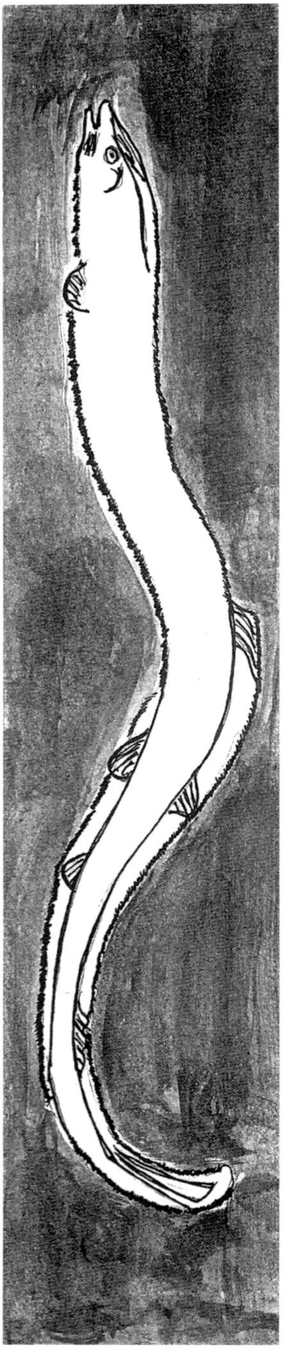

THE FISH TRADERS
AND THE SHIPMEN

The writer of the Domesday Book
Some curious facts reveals:
He reckoned we had fisheries
Of seven thousand eels.

I bet he was a slippery chap,
Prone to exaggeration,
Working for old Conqueror Bill
To maximise taxation.

The Shipman, he of Chaucer's Tales,
A man of great import,
To coin a phrase he was well (h)eeled
And many things he bought.

Not so the poor old fish trader,
A man sometimes maligned
When all his fish were not too fresh -
You know, the 'stinking' kind!

Art Installation number 22

FISH TRADERS AND SHIPMEN

In medieval times the captain or master of a ship was called the Shipman and his crew the mariners. I suppose this applied to boats sailed on the sea, rivers and inland lakes - otherwise, why would Beverley have a Shipmen's Guild? In those days one famous shipman was to be found as one of the pilgrim storytellers in Chaucer's Canterbury Tales.

There was (and is now) a definite distinction between fishmongers and fishermen - the former sell fish and the latter catch fish to sell. I am not sure where fish traders fit in (you will note The Trail has a separate exhibit for fish traders and fishmongers). Perhaps the fish traders were the wholesalers and the fishmongers were the retailers? You tell me.

What of the derivation of fishmongers? The Latin words mango and mangoneum respectively mean dealer and displayer of wares. The Greek word manganon means a way of bewitching or charming! The implication being that a fishmonger was not always to be trusted! Not quite as bad as Shakespeare's usage: 'Excellent well; you are a fishmonger' - Hamlet to Polonius, Hamlet Act 2, Scene 2. Here the implication is 'flesh monger' or pimp!! I suppose while on this theme we should mention Molly Malone - her of the famous Irish song - whose daytime job was selling fish though at night she was a prostitute.

Read the article in Old Church History from where I learned these gems.

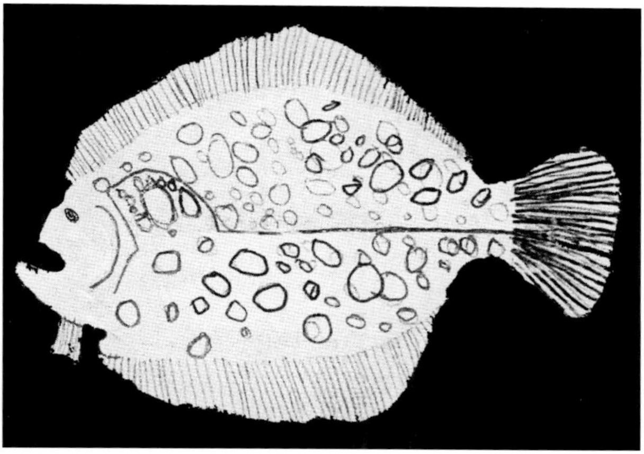

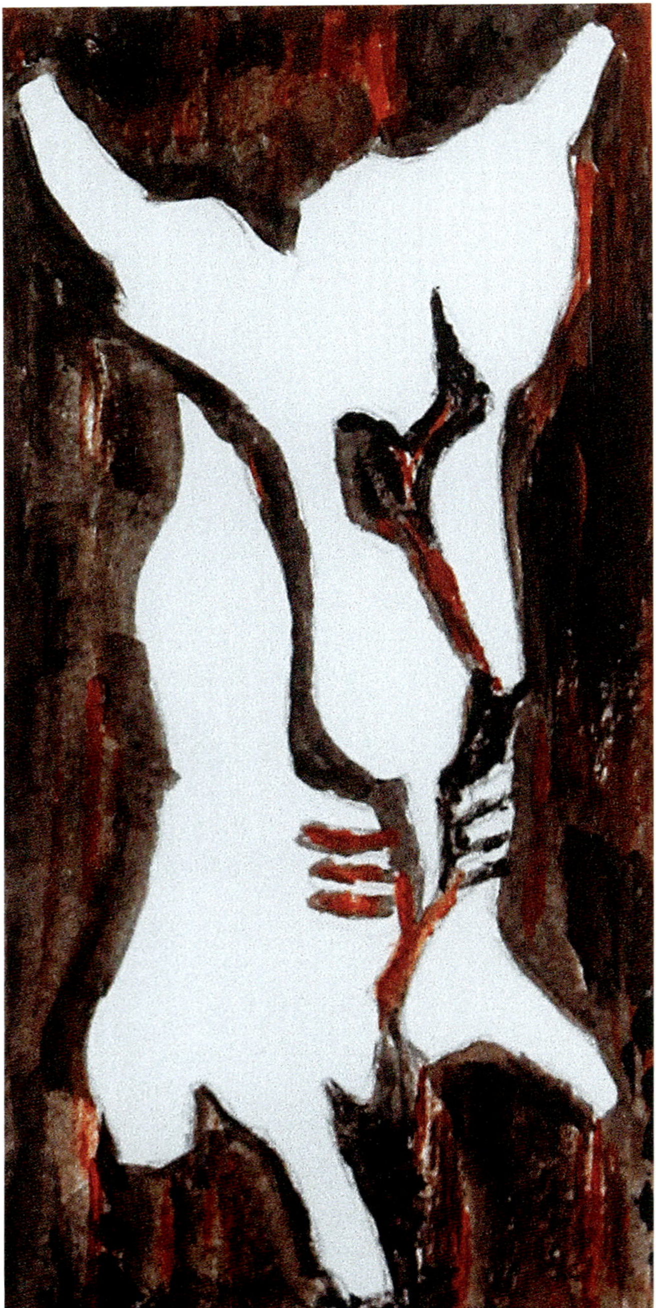

THE BUTCHERS

There was plenty of business down Old Butcher Row,
Though the standards of hygiene were probably low
And some of the details you'd rather not know.

But they'd fairly strong rules which must be obeyed,
Like the banning of maggoty meat, I'm afraid,
And they couldn't sell beef to the rest of the trade.

But the tanners of Beverley were hungry for hides
And the town's chandlers and others besides
Could use the by-products of their oxicides.

So the butchers of Beverley were men of their Age -
In The Mystery Plays they took centre stage
And the Roast Beef of England earned them a good wage.

THE BUTCHERS

The medieval butcher slaughtered animals and prepared and cut meat and fowl. He worked from either a shop in the town or a stall at the local market. It should be remembered that meat was a food for the wealthy and was rarely part of the diet of the poor. If you could afford it a huge variety was available including pork, lamb, veal, venison, goat, poultry, rabbit, hare, swan, heron, peacock and even bear, squirrel and hedgehog*. Beef was not eaten too often, as the cattle were expensive to buy and feed, and were mainly used to provide milk.

Conditions in the large towns and cities were often unhygienic and dirty, and with no means of keeping the meat fresh it was best consumed on the day of slaughter. In his poem, Hickory alludes to the purveying of old and maggoty meat - though, except in the very big cities, this did not seem to happen very often, otherwise the butcher would soon lose his reputation or be severely punished - dragged through the streets, covered in excrement, made to drink sour beer and slung in the stocks, as the historian Annie Grey tells us.

Most of us, at one time or another, will have walked down The Shambles in York, probably not realising it was once lined with butchers' shops with slaughterhouses in the back; nor that at one time the word 'shambles' referred to the tables in the butchers' shops.

*Just as an aside, many years ago I was invited to a traveller's caravan for lunch, where I consumed what I thought was a chicken sandwich - later to find out it was roasted hedgehog cooked in an earthenware pot. It was delicious!

Rembrandt's Slaughtered Ox In The Louvre, Paris since 1857
Courtesy: wikimedia commons

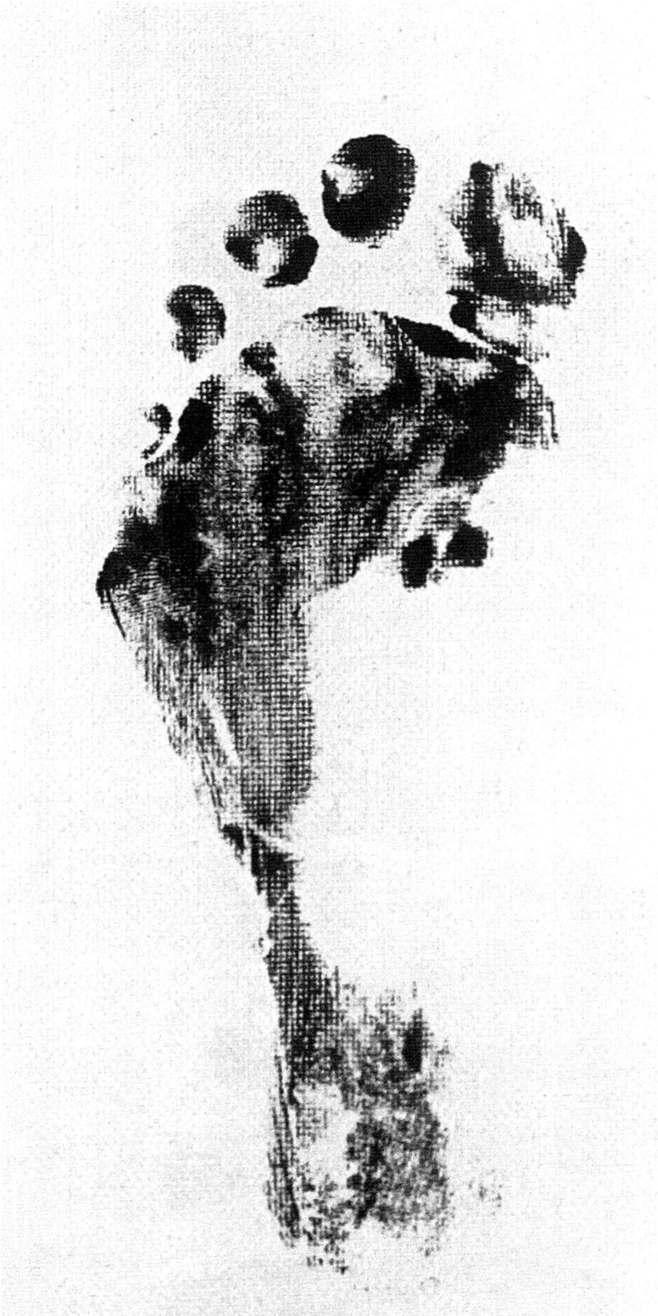

THE WALKERS

Of all the medieval trades
That plied in Walkergate,
It is perhaps the strangest one
We've come across to date.

For here the newly woven cloth
Was brought to clean and check
By washing in the waters of
The, so called, Walker Beck.

The cloth would then be trod upon
To soften or to shrink it
And cleanse it of impurities,
Tho' unlikely you may think it.

It might not be the greatest job
For fame and for renown,
But they had, it could be said,
The cleanest feet in town.

THE WALKERS and THE FULLERS

When the wool comes off the sheep it is first woven into a loose fibre but is left covered in grease. The next stage is fulling, which involves first scouring or cleaning the wool fibre, and then milling, which makes it thicker. These tasks were carried out in Roman and early medieval times by walkers or fullers - until the process was automated by using watermills.

Now here's the thing: the fullers were highly ranked, along with the leech collectors and the lime burners, as having the most terrible jobs (*see table opposite*).

So why was that then? The scouring or cleansing involved seven to eight hours of pounding the wool, using your feet in a big wooden bowl filled with human urine. The urine had been left to mature for a couple of weeks so that it had a rich content of ammonia to clean out the grease. So here we have the poor old fuller jumping up and down for a few hours and breathing in the noxious ammonia fumes while he did so. Later, Fuller's Earth replaced urine, but it was still a stinky job!

THE MEDIEVAL LABOUR EXCHANGE: WORST JOBS AVAILABLE

THE LEECH COLLECTOR: leeches were used for blood letting - thought to be therapeutic in the middle ages . The leech collectors waded through infested river and streams , acting like live bait, allowing the leeches to fix on their legs When they had got enough, they pulled 'em off and put them in a bucket to sell to the barber surgeon.

THE LIME BURNER: limestone was extracted from a quarry and burned at very high temperatures [> 1000 degrees C] in a lime kiln to make it soft and malleable [quick lime] for building, rendering, plastering and lime washing. The kilns were looked after by the lime burner often working for 48 hours at a time. The quick lime stank as did the workers- there was danger too as the hot chalk dust could explode.

THE WHIPPING BOY: this unfortunate young man was educated alongside a Royal Prince in Renaissance Europe Unfortunately when the prince transgressed the poor whipping boy took the punishment.

THE SIN EATER: this person sat alongside the body of a recently deceased and partook of a meal of food and drink . It was thought that the dead person's sins transferred to the Sin Eater. Amongst the superstitious people of the Middle ages they were not popular as they were loaded up with other people's sins

THE GONG FARMER: In Tudor times there was a group of workers called gong or night time workers. Under the cover of darkness they went around clearing excrement from the cess pits and privies and transporting it to dumps outside the city- while the city slumbered on!

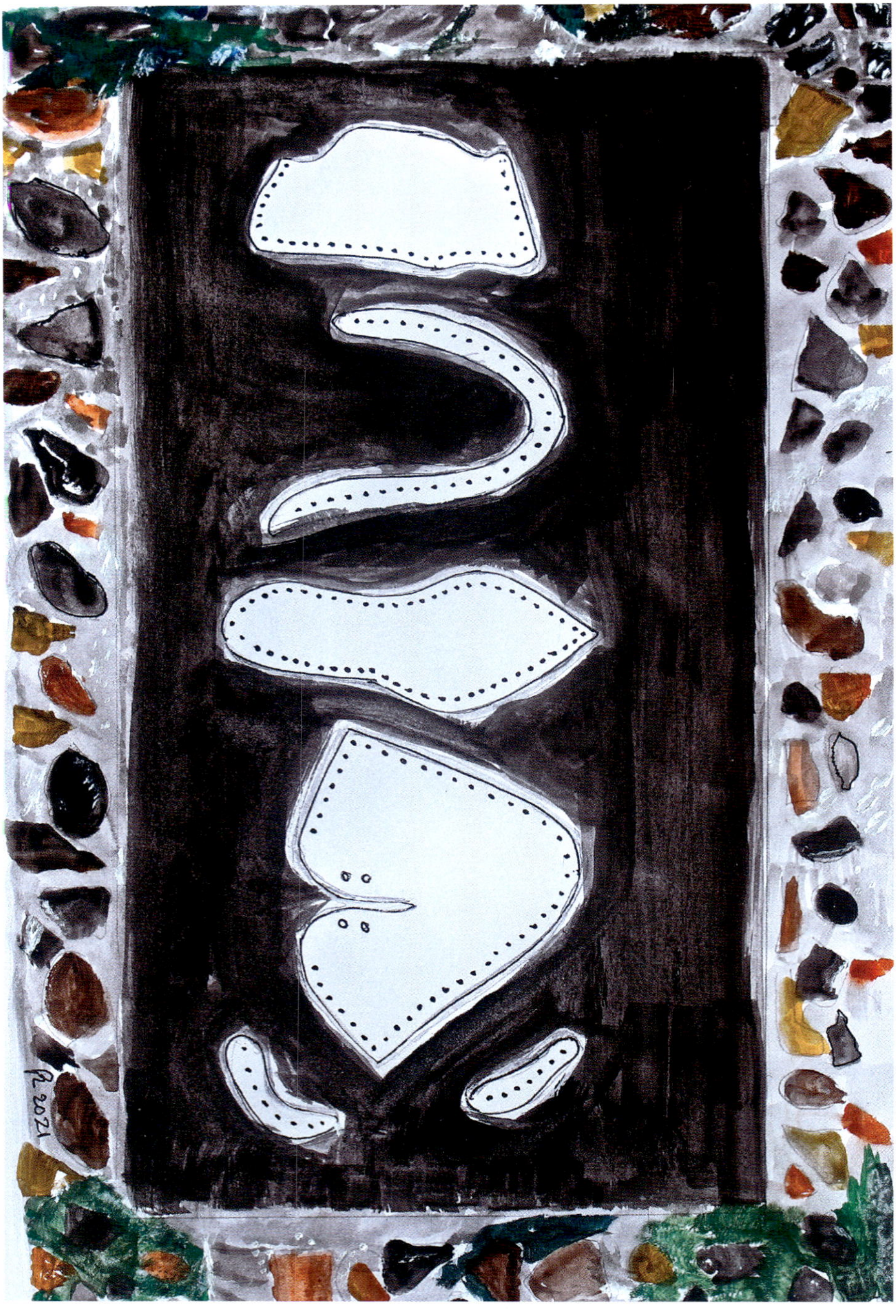

THE CORDWAINERS

The aficionados of your local pub quiz
Are the ones who might know what a cordwainer is,
And should you perchance find one of them sober
He'll tell you the name derives from Cordoba
In Spain.

In Spain, at the time when the Moors still held sway
In Andalucia, because it was they
Who discovered the art of making fine leather -
The smartest of guys, no doubt whatever,
In Spain.

Meantime the shoemakers of the East Riding
Were quick off the mark in jointly deciding
The cordwainer brand would make them top dogs
And earn them more groats for each pair of clogs,
In Yorkshire.

THE CORDWAINERS

The cordwainer is a shoemaker who makes new shoes from new leather. The term is derived from the old French *cordonier*, a shoemaker who originally worked only with 'cordwan' or 'cordvan' leather from Spain. He is not to be confused with the much inferior cobbler, who only mends shoes and is not allowed to be a member of the Cordwainers' Guild, but is occasionally allowed to make shoes from old leather. Perhaps the cordwainers, annoyed at being associated with cobblers originated the term 'cobbled together' to mean a substandard job! The reason for the expression 'the cobblers' children go ill-shod' is because they were so poor, they could not afford shoes for their own children.

The cordwainer worked almost exclusively with leather obtained from the local tannery. He worked with a variety of instruments: awls, knives, hammers, pincers and rasps. When you look at the shoe patterns in the road opposite Tesco, like me you may be a little bit flummoxed as to how the shoe may be produced - well, I think it is a 'medieval turn shoe' or 'boot' which was simply sewn together, shrunk in water and then turned inside out. Look at my drawings opposite but if you are none the wiser, spend a few minutes watching *'Making Medieval Turn Shoes'* on YouTube.

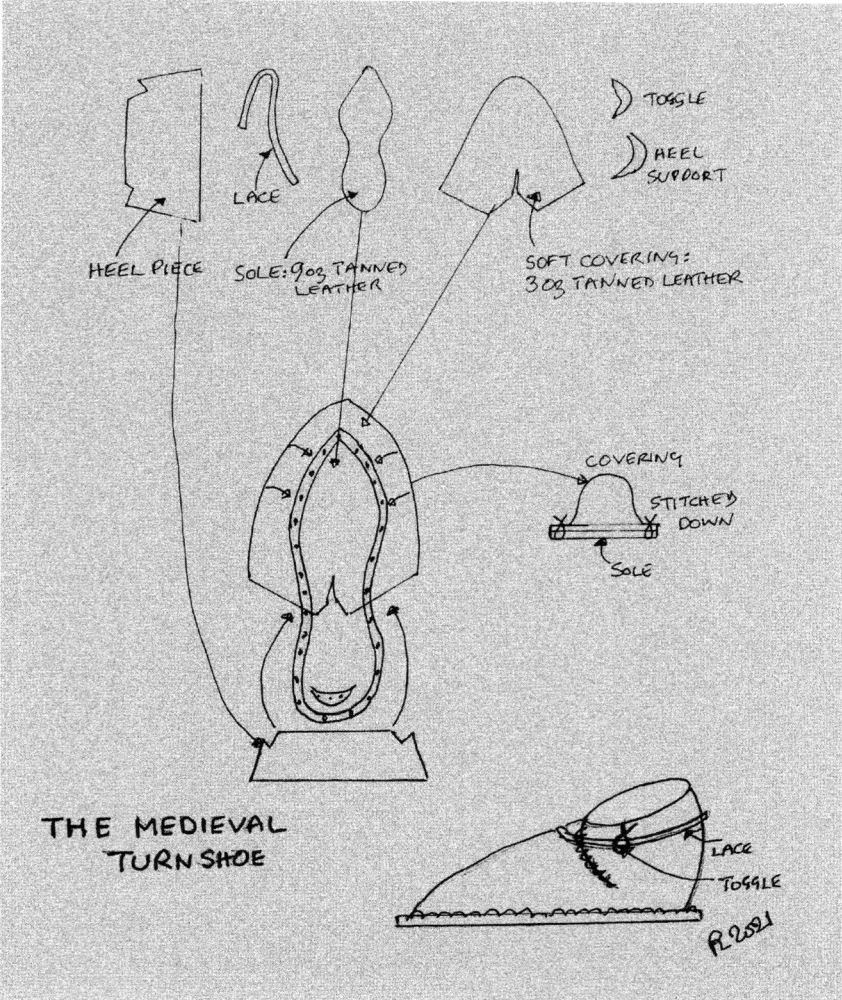

HEEL PIECE

LACE

SOLE: 9oz TANNED LEATHER

TOGGLE

HEEL SUPPORT

SOFT COVERING: 3oz TANNED LEATHER

COVERING

STITCHED DOWN

SOLE

THE MEDIEVAL TURN SHOE

LACE

TOGGLE

R 2021

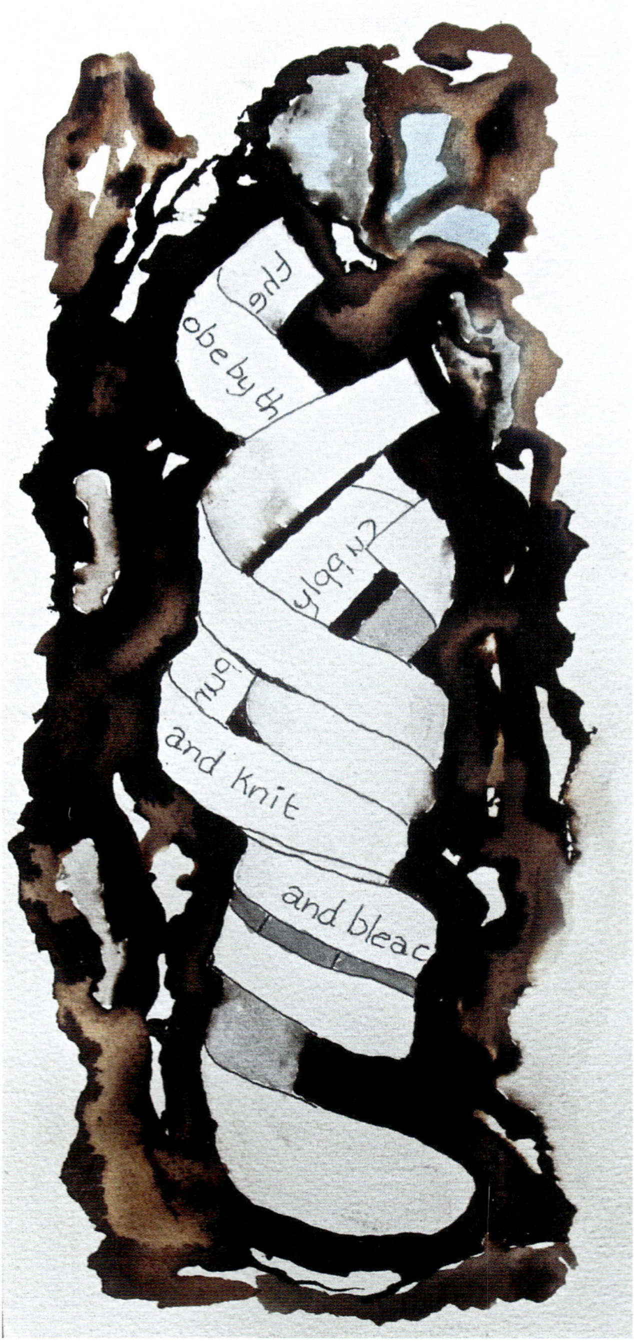
obe by th
and knit
and bleac

THE SPINNERS

The spinner was part of that age old process
As the fleece was transmogrified into the dress
By the shearer, the carder and the comber, I guess,
Until the spun thread could reach the seamstress.

The spinner a woman, invariably so -
Worked from her cottage, her wages were low
But at least she didn't have too far to go.

No, she probably didn't have to travel too far
But her hours would be long and you know what men are
When she wanted some help he'd be off for a jar.

So it was no surprise, with the world all against her,
No prospect of marriage in Beverley Minster,
That many a spinner ended up as a spinster.

THE SPINNERS and THE SPINSTERS

Definitions :

Spinning is an ancient textile art in which animal, plant or synthetic fibres are drawn out and twisted to form yarn. A female who spins is called a **spinster** and a man who spins is called a **spinner.** Only in the C17th did the word spinster acquire the connotation of an unmarried woman who spins.

Some Facts:

In the Middle Ages there were far more women who spun than men. Often the husband would be the weaver. A single woman had a much higher output because she did not have other household duties. The married spinsters were true multitaskers - there are paintings that show them spinning while out walking, riding and tending to the livestock.

Handspinning or **drop spinning** was the norm until the late medieval times when the spinning wheel (Great Wheel or Walking Wheel) was introduced. The **spindle** was a short wooden stick with a whorl or weight at the bottom made out of a stone or clay. The **distaff** is a rod or pole forked at the top to hold the ball of wool. One square metre of fabric requires some three thousand metres of spun thread. A dress required between three and five square metres of cloth. The spinster spun at between forty and one hundred metres per hour. Even if she spun at two hundred metres per hour it would take forty-five **hours** to make the cloth for the dress!! (Facts from Katrin Kania).

Industrialisation of spinning did not come until the C17th, when Hargreaves's **spinning jenny** and John Kay's **flying shuttle** revolutionised matters.

Just in case you don't have The Trail guide with you and are wondering about the inscription - well it is one very small part of a poem by James Coates which goes on for pages and pages. I think the poem is called *Bridlington Quay* and was written in 1813.

'Their wardrobe by themselves supplied,
They spun and knit and bleach'd and dy'd:
Their clothes and food alike were plain
Such as our moderns would disdane'.

Don't tell anyone but there is a small mistake on the 'Spiral' inscription - it says 'supply' which should have been 'supplied'.

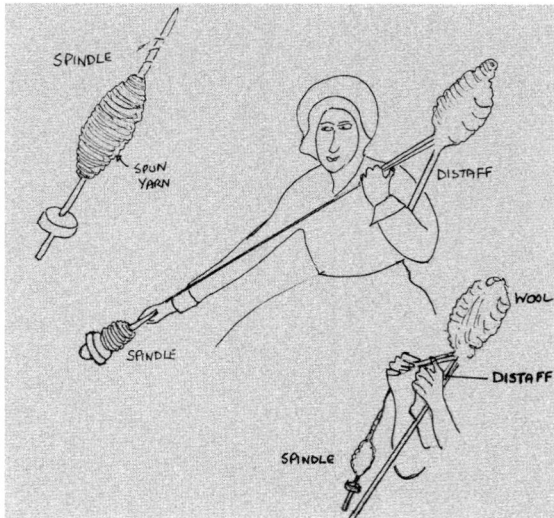

MADDER

THE DYERS

As you walk into town along Dyer Lane,
If you've found a place for your car,
Stop for a moment to consider the name
And to imagine where you are.

For here's where the Dyers were dyeing the cloth
With natural primary dyes
Like the weld for the yellow, the madder for red
And the woad as blue as her eyes.

The blue became known as the Beverley Blue
Wherever our cloth might be sent,
And brought much renown to Beverley Town
In the markets of Bruges and Ghent.

The Dyers were men at the top of their game,
Leaders of style and of fashion,
Working their vats with a positive aim
With purpose and pride and with passion.

THE DYERS

York has red and purple; Lincoln has green, scarlet and grey; Coventry has blue and Beverley blue and red. So, what's this then? Their teams' football colours? No, indeed not. In the C11th these were the colours of dyestuffs which these towns or cities were licensed by law to make and use.

indigo blue

madder red dyed wool

Natural dyes came from various sources:

red - madder root (Rubia tinetorum), kermes or grana from insects

blue - woad leaves (Isatia tinctoria)

violet - orchil from lichen

crimson - brasilwood from the East India tree

purple - brasilwood from the East India tree

yellow - weld, dyers› rocket, turmeric, saffron, onion skin, marigold, chamomile

green - indigo, weld, turmeric

brown - walnut shells, bark

The three staples of the medieval dyeing industry were weld (yellow), madder (red) and woad (blue). The red dye which came from madder was significantly more expensive than the blue dye which came from woad. The root nature of the madder plant meant the red dye was only harvested once a year, whereas the leaves of the woad plant could be gathered several times throughout the year, making more of it available. The dye extracted from woad is 'indigo' - the same dye as is extracted from the foreign indigo plant Indigofera tinctoria, but in lower concentration. It was only in the C20th that plant sources of indigo were replaced by synthetically created dyes.

So what's this **mordant** thing we hear about? Well, mordants were extensively used in the medieval dyeing industry to open the wool fibres and allow the dye pigment to bond onto the fibres. This made the colour more permanent, as well as making it water and light 'fast'. The different mordants were also instrumental in deciding the shade, tone, intensity and final colour of the cloth. Those used were alum (a volcanic mineral salt), clubmoss and iron oxide which created dark reds and browns.

When did the dyeing take place? Sometimes the wool was dyed after the initial washing with soap and water. This was called 'dyed-in-the-wool' or pre-dyeing - if dyed at this stage the wool would always retain its basic colour. Hence the term 'a dyed-in-the-wool Tory'! The alternative and probably most frequently used method was to dye the cloth after it had been woven, fulled and walked.

THE TAILOR'S THIMBLE

R 2021

THE TAILORS

Before the days of the ready made suit,
Before the Montague Burton,
You didn't require the fifty bob
For clothes to go to work in.

You followed your Dad, as he'd followed his,
In their line of craft or trade;
And you wore their smocks and their overalls
And their best coat for the Parade.

While the tailor made the finest clothes
For the Master and the Dame.
Appropriate to their place in the world
Whenever nobility came.

Before the dawn of the Ready to Wear
Was the age of the Tailor Made,
And one was known by the clothes one wore -
It's as simple as that I'm afraid.

THE TAILORS

The craft's designation is a common surname in many languages: *Taylor* in English, *Couturier* in French, *Sneider* in German, *Sarti* in Italian, *Terzi* in Turkish and *Darzi* in Hindi or Urdu. So, there were a lot of tailors about, but you must remember that, certainly in the early medieval times, their services were only available to, and used by, a small number of people. Most simply could not afford them. I have seen it written that clothes had one purpose only and that was to conceal the body - seems a bit farfetched, but you can see the point! Certainly, as the Middle Ages moved on the clothes people wore were an important indicator of wealth and status, and the tailor craftsman was a lucrative and highly paid profession. We are all familiar with the peasants' roughly hewn and stitched knee length 'gowns', and the elegant and exotic costumes and dresses of royalty - but what about peoples' underwear? Well, there was no Marks & Spencer to pop into for a bra and pants or a pair of 'boxers' - so what did people wear?

The 2012 edition of *BBC History* gives us some idea. Men wore a shirt and 'braies' - underpants somewhat similar to today's shorts. These were made of linen or finely woven wool, and often extended from the waist to the knees. Over these breeches were worn, laced up tight and making the act of emptying your bladder a complex and lengthy process - so the cod piece (medieval English for a bag) was invented. Women wore drawers or a chemise, often with no pants but knee length socks! Corsets did not become popular until the C18th. There is evidence that bras - flatteringly called 'breast bags' - were sometimes worn, while on other occasions women flattened their breasts with rectangular strips of cloth called a *strophium* or *mamillare*. So, there you have it. Victoria's Secret eat your heart out!

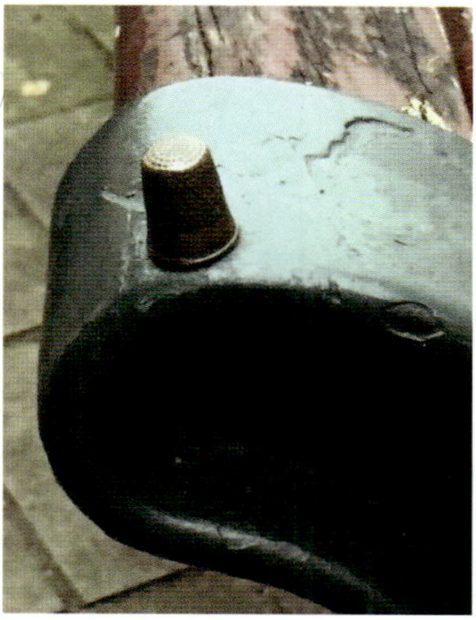

EYEBRIGHT

THE APOTHECARIES

The apothecary, an ancient name,
His was an ancient craft;
Using plants he picked for free,
He clearly wasn't daft.

The feverfew, that could be found
In odd neglected borders,
He testified as just the thing
For headache and womb disorders.

The cinquefoil, on the other hand,
Brought relief and cheer
To those poor souls who suffered from
Attacks of diarrhoea.

The asthma and the chesty cough
Coltsfoot he said would cure,
And eyebright he would recommend
When he was not too sure.

But nowadays, when overuse
Is threatening vital drugs,
The hunt is on for natural ways
Of beating beastly bugs.

THE APOTHECARIES

"Give me an ounce of civet, good apothecary, to sweeten my imagination", says King Lear in Shakespeare's play of the same name. Apothecaries were practising throughout the Middle Ages, and by the C15th and C16th had their own Guild and Livery. The name derives from the Ancient Greek *apotheke* which means a repository or storehouse; but their job, of course, was to provide pills and potions much as a pharmacy does today. In order to practise they had to undergo a long period of training as an apprentice and acquire a detailed knowledge of the plants, herbs and other substances used in their trade. Because they also used imported spices they were occasionally referred to as spicers or pepperers!

It seems to me that if you were ill in medieval times you had a number of choices, largely determined by how much money you had. If you were very poor you might ask your neighbour if he had any remedies growing in his garden which might help. Failing this, you could go to a monastery (they usually had big herb gardens) and ask the monks for help. Next in line might be the 'wise women' who practised a mixture of folk medicine and midwifery. Then came the apothecary, who not only compounded and dispensed the medications which the 'top of the market' physicians and surgeons prescribed, but was also open to the lay public to listen to their symptoms and prescribe a cure. I just loved this extract from the writings of William Bulleyn which shows that, even in those days, Health and Safety and professional jealousy were coming in!

'The apothecary must first serve God. He must foresee the end, be clenly, and pity the poor. His place of dwelling must be clenly, to please the sense withal. His garden must be at hand with plenty of herbs, seeds and roots. He must read Dioscorides. He must have his mortars, stills, pots, filters, glasses, boxes, clean and sweet. He must have two places in his shop, one for the cleanest physick and the base place for chirurgic stuff. He is neither to decrease or diminish the physician's prescriptions. He is to meddle only in his own vocation, and to remember that his office is only the physician's cook'.

By the way, just in case you didn't know it, Dioscorides, a Greek, wrote his *De Materia Medica* treatise in 65AD.

In The Trail Guide we are told about four of the Apothecary's herbs which feature on the pavers in Toll Gavel - and which at the moment are blinking hard to find because of wear and tear:

Feverfew for headaches and womb disorders

Coltsfoot for coughs and asthma

Eyebright for nasal secretions

Cinquefoil for diarrhoea and other stomach complaints

However, not to be outdone, we will list a few more of interest - **henblane** (*Hyoscyamus niger* or stinking nightshade) and **hemlock** (*Conium maculatum*, a highly poisonous weed), for joint pains; **coriander** for fever; and **wormwood** (*Artemisia absinthium*) mixed with **mint** for stomach pains. Lastly, how about this magic potion prescribed by a sorceress called Morgan Le Fay (Fairy) in *The Knight with the Lion*

Take equal amounts of radish, bishop wort, garlic, wormwood, helinium, crop leek and hollowleek. Pound them up, boil them in butter with celandine and red nettle. Keep the mixture in a brass pot until it is dark red in colour. Strain it through a cloth and smear on the forehead or aching joints.

Don't think I'd get very far asking my old friend 'Phil the Pill' for that in Hengate Pharmacy today!

COLTSFOOT

FEVERFEW

CINQUEFOIL

The Barber Surgeon
by Cherry Polglase

THE BARBER SURGEONS

The Barber Surgeon, a coalition -
The hairdresser and the physician
Two branches of but one tradition.

The barber shop, the barber's pole,
At the base the bloody bowl.

The toothpaste stripes of red and white,
In our town a sombre sight.

These were tough inventive guys,
Experienced and worldly wise.

They pulled the teeth, they lanced the boils,
They drew the blood, applied snake oils.

In times of peace, in times of war,
The sick and injured at their door,
Sons of the razor and the saw.

THE BARBER SURGEONS

The art forms on The Trail associated with the barber surgeon are a bronze snake coiled round the top of a green lamp post and, across the street in the entrance of a shop, two white pillars with a black snake around each. Really the white pillars (or poles) should be striped red and white like today's hairdressers' poles. Let us deal with this first.

The barber surgeon had four tasks: cutting hair, pulling teeth, bloodletting and surgery (lancing boils and amputations for example). The poles were put up outside their shop to advertise these skills. The patient gripped a pole to distend the veins and make the process of bloodletting easier. The red and white colours represented the RED (arterial blood) and WHITE (bandages) involved in the bloodletting.

In Europe the poles are just red and white; however in America they are red, white and blue - some suggest that the blue represents 'venous blood', others say it is a symbol of patriotism and a 'nod' to the nation's flag. On top of the pole there might be a basin which would contain leeches which sucked blood. At the bottom was a second bowl to collect the blood. To top it all off, a string of teeth might be hung on the pole to indicate their dental skills.

Now what about the snakes? Well, it has all got to do with the Greek Gods. A pole or staff with one snake wrapped around it is the symbol of ASCLEPIUS, the Greek God of healing - hence its use in medical insignia.

Often the insignia show two snakes wrapped around the staff. This is called the CADUCEUS and was adopted by Hermes the Greek God of commerce and travel (him with the wings on his feet), also called Mercury by the Romans. On his travels he saw two snakes fighting and flung his stick at them. They wrapped around the stick and he liked it so much it became his emblem. The CADUCEUS was adopted by the alchemists as a sign of professionalism. In C20th it was used on the insignia of the American Public Health Service - maybe just to be different from the ASCLEPIUS symbol or maybe to indicate they were more professional - who knows? But what have snakes got to do with medicine? Some say that by being able to shed and regrow their skin snakes represent 'rebirth', others say it is because snake venom can kill and cure. More bizarrely some say its relevance was that the snake was used to pull parasites out of the body (deworming). I like that!

Many of the earlier medieval guilds became liveries. The Barbers' Company was founded in London in 1462 and merged with the Surgeons' Guild in 1540.

The Surgeons split off in 1745 and formed the Royal College of London which in 1843 became The Royal College of Surgeons of England, of which I have proudly been a Fellow for a mere fifty years!

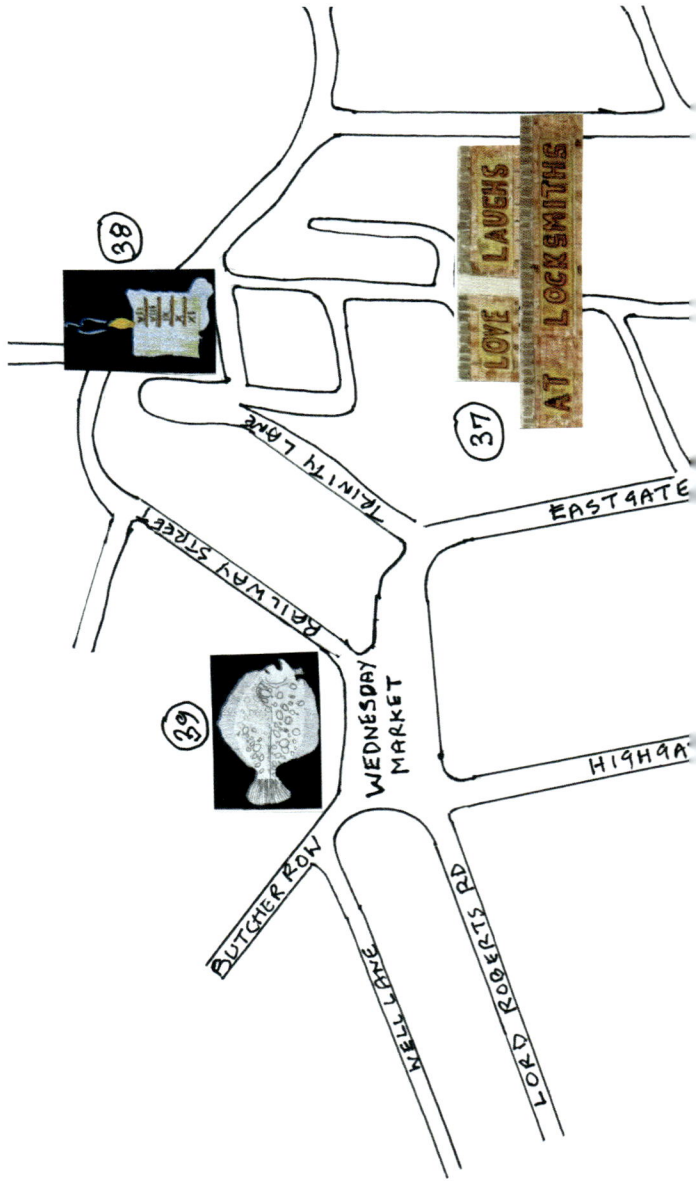

(38)

(37) LOVE LAUGHS AT LOCKSMITHS

(39)

TRINITY LANE

EASTGATE

RAILWAY STREET

WEDNESDAY MARKET

HIGHGA

BUTCHER ROW

WELL LANE

LORD ROBERTS RD

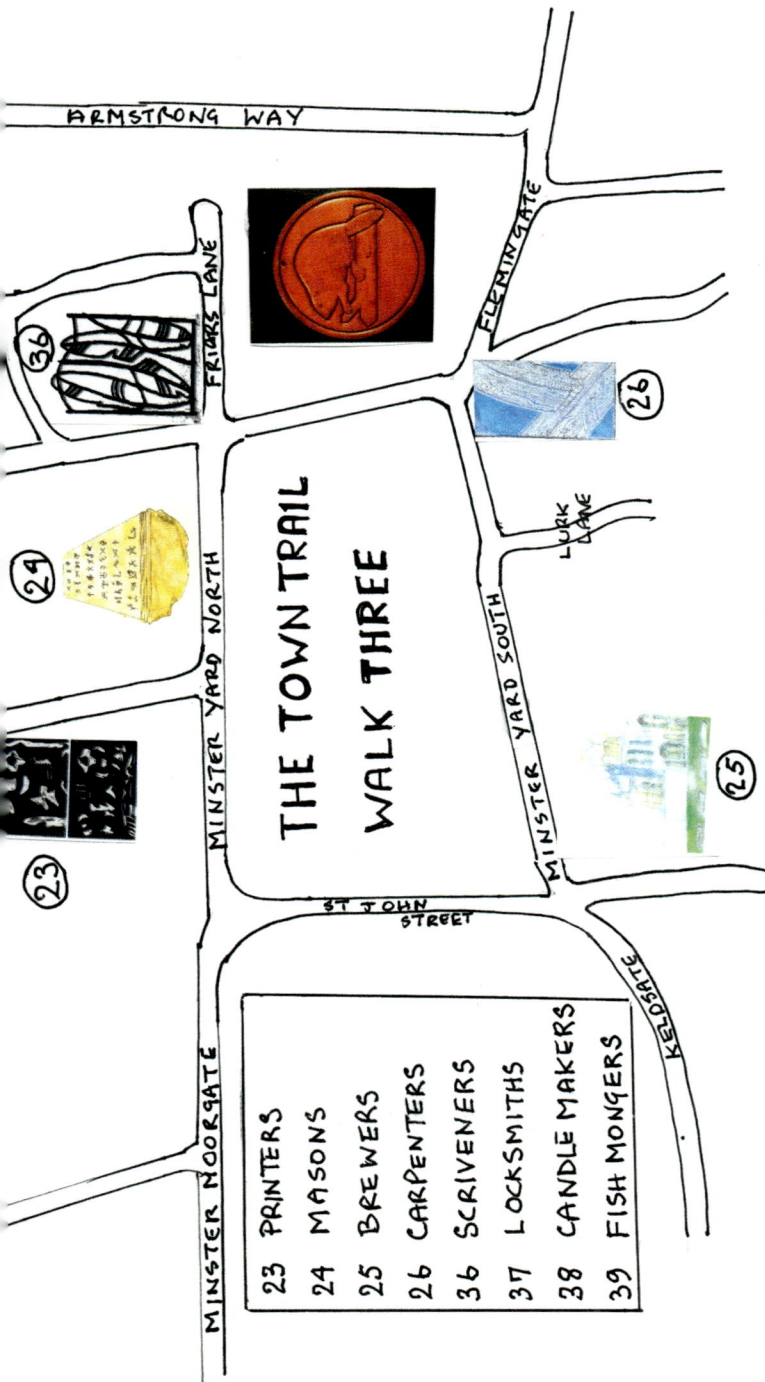

ARMSTRONG WAY

FRIARS LANE

FLEMINGATE

(36)

(26)

LURK LANE

(24)

MINSTER YARD NORTH

THE TOWN TRAIL
WALK THREE

MINSTER YARD SOUTH

(25)

(23)

ST JOHN STREET

KELDGATE

MINSTER MOORGATE

23 PRINTERS
24 MASONS
25 BREWERS
26 CARPENTERS
36 SCRIVENERS
37 LOCKSMITHS
38 CANDLE MAKERS
39 FISH MONGERS

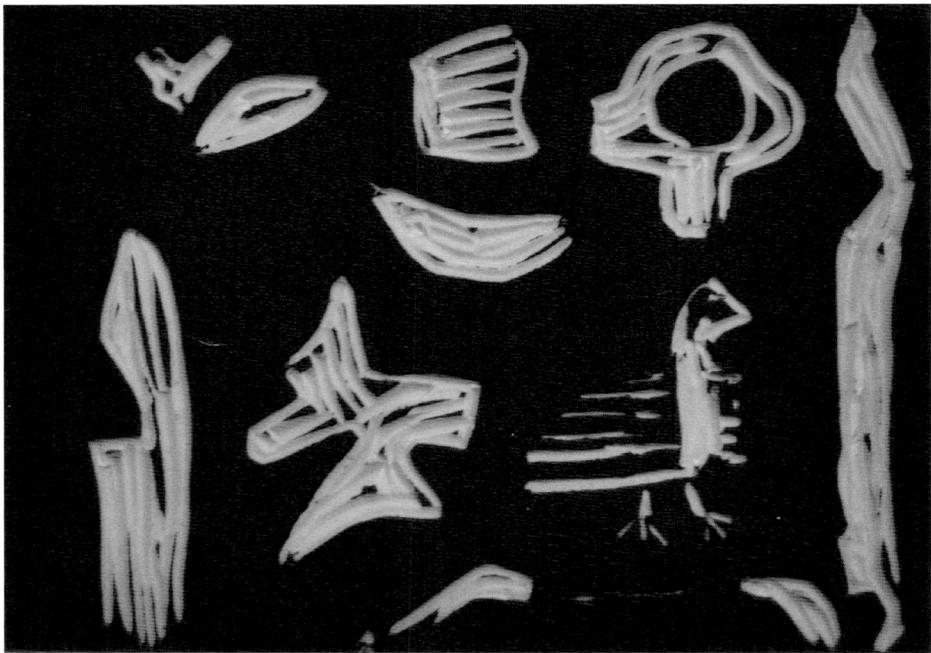

THE PRINTERS

The launching of the Printers Guild, we know with some precision,
Which heralded a brand new world of progress and division.

The founder was a printer's son, nicknamed the Flying Dutchman,
Who could work a printing press and give folk sound instruction.

He started up East Riding Press, from a site in Highgate,
Which no doubt ruffled feathers there and made the scriveners irate.

And then in fifteen hundred and probably sixteen,
He produced a printed book, the first that Beverley'd seen.

The fellow's name was Hugo Goes, a strange old name to use,
Which anglicised in no time became yon 'ugo Goose.

THE PRINTERS

TIMELINE

618-906 AD: Tang Dynasty. Printing is first performed in China using ink on carved wooden blocks.

868 AD: Chinese produce 'Diamond Sutra', the first printed book. The contents of this book, written in Sanskrit, were very important in the Buddhist faith (Vajracchedika).

1241 : The Koreans develop movable type for printing books.

1452 : In Mainz, Germany, Johannes Gutenberg develops a printing press using movable type and produces his illustrated edition of The Bible.

1476 : William Caxton introduces the Gutenberg printing press to England.

1550 : Wallpaper first used in Europe.

So what has this got to do with Beverley? The Printers' 'installation' has been done as a lino cutting. Can you figure out what it is about? Probably not - even though The Trail book tells us it is a fragment of the earliest known English wallpaper, and hung in Christ's College, Cambridge. The person who printed it was Hugo (Hewe) Goes. He was the first known printer of books in the North of England (circa 1509) and worked in Beverley before moving to York. If you look very carefully at the top line of the top cutting, in the middle you will see a symbol resembling an 'H', and if you look at the bottom line on the right there is a symbol of a bird. These are Hugo Goes' signature marks (H for Hugo and the bird for Goes, or Goose).

But what on earth are the rest of the hieroglyphics? The answer lies in looking at a reproduction of the segment of wallpaper from Christ's College shown below. The wallpaper is the last remaining segment from a room used by Lady Margaret Beaufort as her bedchamber. Sure enough the marks of Hugo Goes are present (arrowed, H on left and goose on right). All the shapes on the Beverley installation can be seen making up the design of the wallpaper (said to be a Pomegranate design). It is interesting to note that, at that time, Lady Margaret's confessor was Bishop John Fisher of Flemingate, Beverley.

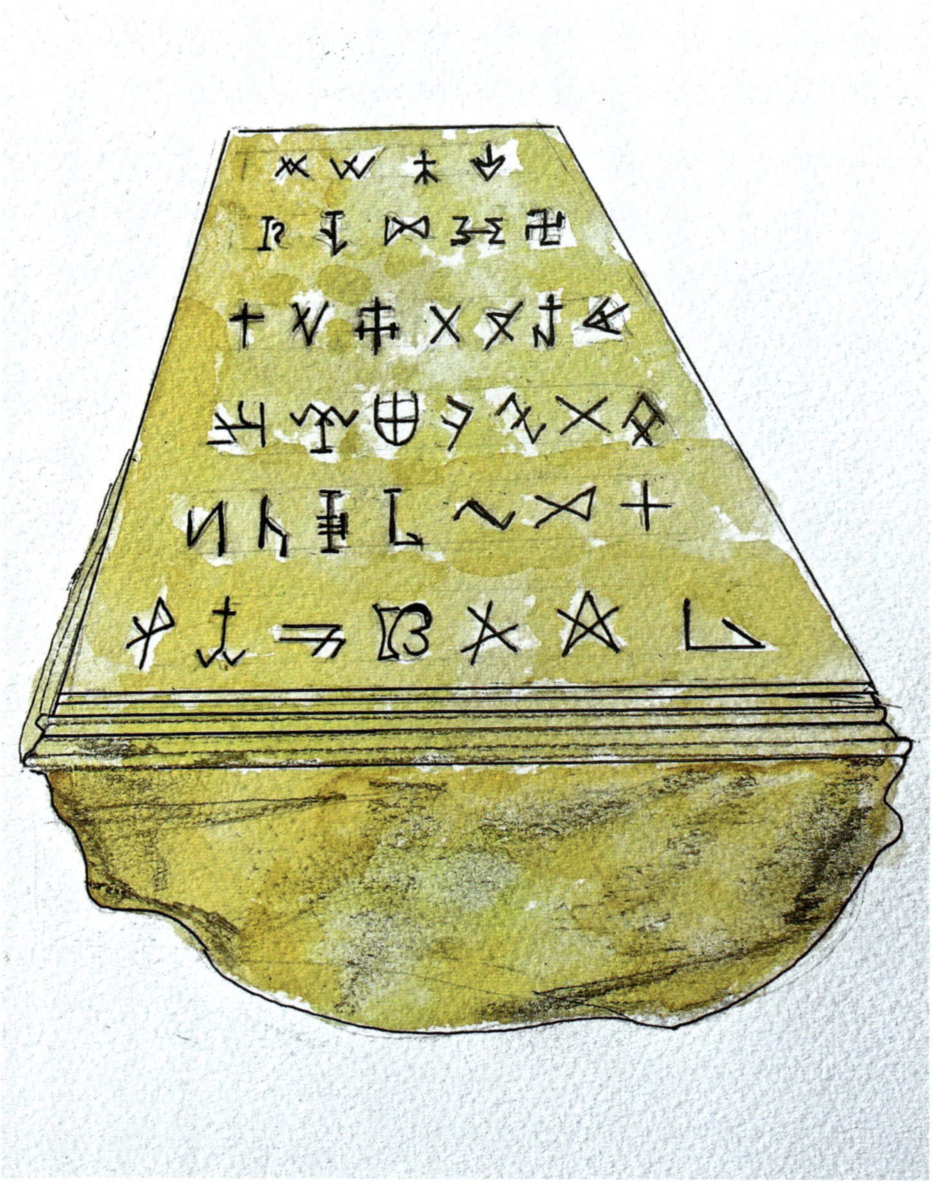

THE MASONS

Its hard to penetrate the world
Of Medieval Masons,
Who'd spend a lifetime on one job,
That took some dedication.

It took some nerve, it took some skill,
It took some perseverance.
But they'd worked at the cutting edge
Of contemporary man's experience.

Just spend a quiet hour or two
In the Minster or St Mary's.
Lift your eyes and bend your knees
Of what you'll be aware is:

That this, which was a building site
For countless generations,
Is now the glorious masterpiece
Of Medieval Masons.

THE STONE MASONS

The apprenticeship of a mason began at the quarry. Here he would learn the skill of splitting stone into transportable rocks. Here experienced masons would carve cut stone into set designs. Having served as an apprentice for several years, the mason became a journeyman and travelled the country seeking work.

Once a decision had been taken to build a church, the design of the building would be worked out in full on tracing floors covered in soft plaster (such a floor still exists at York Minster).

In overall control of the construction of a church was the master mason. When seeking employment, a skilled craftsman could show his future employers an example of his work. However, a stone mason would present his 'masterpiece' (i.e. an example of his work) to his employer or Guild members and answer certain questions. His answers would demonstrate his skill and knowledge as a craftsman. Once employed, the master mason had many responsibilities: he was an architect, a builder, a designer, an engineer and an organiser.

The stone mason needed to adapt to changes in architectural style. Towards the end of the 12th century the semi-circular arch and massive stone pillars of the Norman period were replaced by the pointed arch and single lancet windows (so named for being in the shape of a lance). A century later buttresses supported walls and thus larger window openings became possible. The windows were often built with elaborate flamboyant tracery. In 14th and 15th centuries flying buttresses helped take the weight of the roof. This allowed for the building of even larger windows. Here vertical lines of stone, carried to the top of the windows gave support for the placing of stained glass between the mullions. Generally, churches became taller and were filled with light.

Built over several centuries, medieval churches retain a harmony of style and beauty which can be seen in every direction in which they are viewed. They continue to show the skill and dedication of generations of stone masons who devoted their lives, often working in dangerous conditions, knowing that they would never live to see the completed building.

The Town Trail stone representing the Guild of Masons shows a number of masons marks found in the church which represent the hundreds of stone masons who came to the wealthy town of Beverley. For here pilgrims and kings provided money for the re-building of Beverley Minster (the burial place of St John of Beverley) and merchants, made rich by the wool trade, provided money for the building of a church dedicated to St Mary; a place where members of the guilds could gather. Today we are fortunate in being able to visit churches, many begun more than eight hundred years ago, which are still intact and used for their original purpose.

JOHN BARLEYCORN

They laid him down three furrows deep
Laid clots upon his head
The three men made a solemn vow
John Barleycorn is dead

They let him lie for a very long time
Till the rain from heaven did fall
Then little Sir John sprang up his head
And did amaze them all

They let him stand till midsummers day
Then he looked both pale and wan
Then little Sir John he grew a long beard
And so became a man

They hired men with scythes so sharp
To cut him off at the knee
They rolled and tied him round the waist
They served him barbarously

The hired men with crab tree sticks
To cut him skin from bone
And the miller he's served him worse than that
For he's ground him between two stones

They worked their will on John Barleycorn
But he lived to tell the tale
For they pour him out of an old brown jug
And they called him home brewed ale

Olde English Folksong

54

THE BREWERS

In thirteen hundred and seventy one,
Which is quite a long time ago,
The Trail historians have unearthed some facts
Which are of interest to know.

You could buy a gallon of Beverley beer
For one and a half present day pence,
But the cost of a pint I cannot work out
For it really doesn't make sense.

No wonder young people were plied with ale,
Just imagine your beer swilling daughter.
But the everyday wisdom of those times
Said it's safer than drinking water!

For the beer was inspected for quality and price
And checked that you got a full measure,
And so in a world that was not all nice
The bitter was something to treasure.

THE BREWERS

The 'art piece' dedicated to The Brewers is one of the more unusual on The Trail. Set into the grassy verge opposite the south transept of The Minster are six flagstones with the words of an Old English folksong '*John Barleycorn Must Die*' engraved on them. The words of the song were first published as a poem in 1568, and in 1782 the great Robbie Burns published his own version, which you must look at (Google John Barleycorn, wiki). You may well ask what all this has to do with brewing - as indeed I did when I first saw the stones. In writing and poetry when human characteristics are given to a non-human entity it is called 'personification'. In this case, the words of *John Barleycorn Must Die* are a personification of the process of growing the crop barley and turning it into beer and whisky. The serial (no pun intended) indignities which Barleycorn suffers represent what happens to the barley on its way to being made into 'the drink'.

Thus: 'They've plowed, they've sown, they've harrowed him in, thrown clods upon his head' represents the planting or sowing of the barley.

And: 'They've hired men with their scythes so sharp to cut him off at the knee' represents the harvesting or reaping of the barley.

It is suggested that the song was originally written to serve as a warning against alcohol but Robbie Burn's version makes John a hero!

Clever stuff, eh? Get onto YouTube and listen to Stevie Winwood of Traffic playing the song on acoustic guitar. The words will have new meaning.

Herttel Pyprew [brewer] from
House Book of Mendel, 1475
Creative Commons.

THE CARPENTERS

The carpenter, the joiner and their chums the cabinet makers
Might be described as woodworkers, as were the undertakers.

The joiner did the joinery, he made and hung the doors,
The architraves, the skirting boards, he laid the timber floors.

The cabinet maker was the guy with the greatest skills,
He'd make you anything you want, if you could pay his bills.

The carpenter did the heavy work, he built the timber frames
For the Merchants' houses and the folk with well known names.

And when the King's librarian came, he found things pretty good:
Beverley being rather large and ''welle builded of wood''.

THE CARPENTERS

"If I were a carpenter and you were a lady

Would you marry me anyway?

If I worked my hands in wood,

Would you still love me?".

Listen to the words of Tim Hardin's 1967 hit song - or, if you prefer, listen to Johnny Cash sing it with his wife June Carter Cash (1970). The lyrics might well be about a medieval carpenter. The carpenter was a well-respected and highly skilled craftsman and well paid 'to boot.' He might have a workshop in town where he crafted everyday essentials such as buckets, tools, furniture, windows and doors; he might have a bigger workspace where he made timber frames and arches, disassembled them and sent them off to the building sites. He might work with a particular stonemason making his ladders, hoists and scaffolding, or he might be an 'itinerant' structural carpenter who travelled the country helping to build the houses and churches of that time.

The tools of a medieval carpenter and joiner were many and varied: hatchets for cutting and trimming, saws, drawknives for trimming, adzes for cutting, shaping and smoothing, gimlets, augers or awls (drill bits for making holes). Not forgetting braces, chisels and gouges, planes, crowbars, hammers - and of course a compass, square, ruler and divider, as much of his work was precision based.

The Town Trail art exhibit for The Carpenters demonstrates a 'mortice and tenon' joint - the most commonly used method of joining wood because it was the strongest. Note the joint was fixed with wooden pegs - the medieval carpenter rarely used nails. Also employed were 'dovetail' joints and 'scarf' joints - the latter when two pieces of wood were joined to make a longer beam.

Finally a few words on the 'marks' used by carpenters. These might be simple letters to show who had crafted the piece, or signs for correct positioning of a particular beam or frame, but my favourites are the 'burns marks' which look like large cigarette burns and which were left by the superstitious craftsman to symbolise protection from the ever-present risk of fire in wood-framed buildings.

Taper burn marks at Haddon Hall (Wiki CC}

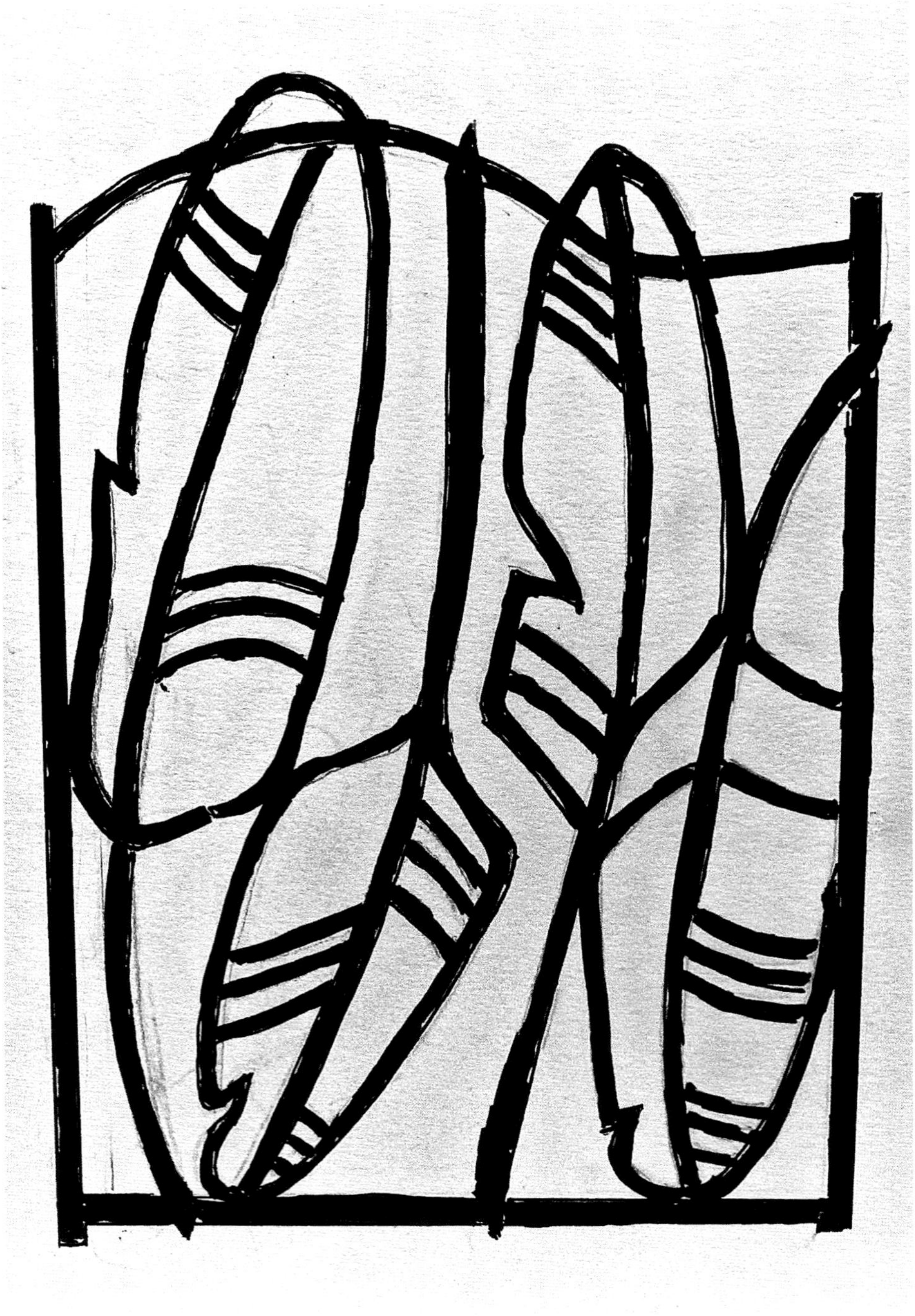

THE SCRIVENERS

For long years of my life I was troubled because
I never quite knew what a scrivener was.

I guessed it had something to do with hand writing
But fairly dull stuff, nothing exciting.

And so it turns out they were literary hacks,
The Middle Age version of our bureaucrats.

They wrote things in Latin and the French of the day
Which needed recording in an authorised way.

They were orderly chaps, these men of the quill,
In Brussels, I think, you will find a few still.

THE SCRIVENERS

I didn't know what 'scrivener' meant - do you?

When I first looked at The Scrivener's Gate it took me a while to figure out it was four quills (pens) cleverly aligned - what about you? I wasn't sure what The Scrivener's Gate had to do with the entrance to Beverley Friary, and why it was placed there. Do you know?

A scrivener was a medieval scribe who, because he could read and write, made his living by writing and copying documents. Remember in the Middle Ages the average person could neither read nor write - so they would take their letter to a stall at the local fair or market and ask the 'itinerant' scrivener to read it for them, and if necessary pen a reply - using, of course, a quill and ink. The other people who could read and write were the nuns and the monks, and indeed until the C11th and C12th most books and manuscripts were produced in the monasteries and kept in their libraries - hence The Scrivener's Gate is appropriately placed at the entrance to the Beverley Dominican Friary. Now we have explained these facts let us consider one or two more questions.

What did the scriveners write on? Papyrus, made of Egyptian reeds, was used until the C7th or C8th when the percamenarius, or parchment maker, started to make parchment out of animal skins. Parchment and vellum are generally regarded as the same thing, but strictly speaking vellum is only made from calfskin (veal or French *veau*). Making the parchment is a skilled and tedious process - the sheep, cow or goat skins had to be first washed in cold water for up to twenty-four hours, and the hair was then loosened by soaking in lime and water for several days. The hide was then hung over a 'beam' and the hair scraped away with a long curved knife. Next, the skin was stretched over a wooden frame, attached to it by strings and pegs which were constantly tightened to keep the skin taut. The skin was initially kept wet with hot water and then scraped again with a special knife called a 'lunellum' - designed to avoid making holes. Finally, it was allowed to dry, scraped again to the requisite thickness and then released and rolled up - et voila! A parchment or vellum roll! Paper came into use in about the C15th and was made of linen pulp - called rag paper - and very strong and durable it was, too.

What did the scriveners write with? Of course, they wrote with feathers or quills. The best were from the goose or swan - preferably the outer pinion or flight feathers. These are long and have a slight curve on them which, if from the left-hand wing, fit nicely between the thumb and forefinger of the scrivener - who incidentally always wrote right-handed. Some of the feathers were stripped from the quill, which was then hardened by dipping in hot sand. Finally, the 'nib' was formed by cutting the quill end with a knife – yes, indeed, a 'pen knife'. The quills needed constant resharpening and for a busy day's work the scrivener may have had 60 -100 preprepared quills!

What did the scriveners use as ink? There were basically two sorts of ink - carbon ink made of charcoal or lampblack mixed with gum, and then the much more interesting 'gall' inks made from oak apples. These looked like big berries and formed on the oak tree when a gall wasp laid its egg on a growing bud. When the 'apples' were crushed up and mixed with ferrous sulphate, water and gum arabic, the tannic acid released from the apple produced a black liquid which was boiled down to form a fairly viscous ink. Red ink was very common in medieval manuscripts and was made by grinding vermillion (mercuric sulphide) with egg white and gum. Lastly an anecdote which signifies that life as a scribe was not all plain sailing. It is said that the scribe Adam Pankhurst, who was copyist to Geoffrey Chaucer of the Canterbury Tales, made so many errors that Chaucer threatened him with the curse of an outbreak of 'scabs' unless his performance improved!

The old gate way into the Dominican Friary

The green plaque (middle left) states "this gateway is of early 16C date and formed part of the enclosure wall of the Dominican Friary founded in the middle of 13C and suppressed in 1599. The gate way was moved bodily from the other side of Eastgate in 1964 to ensure permanent preservation". (courtesy Beverley Civic Society)

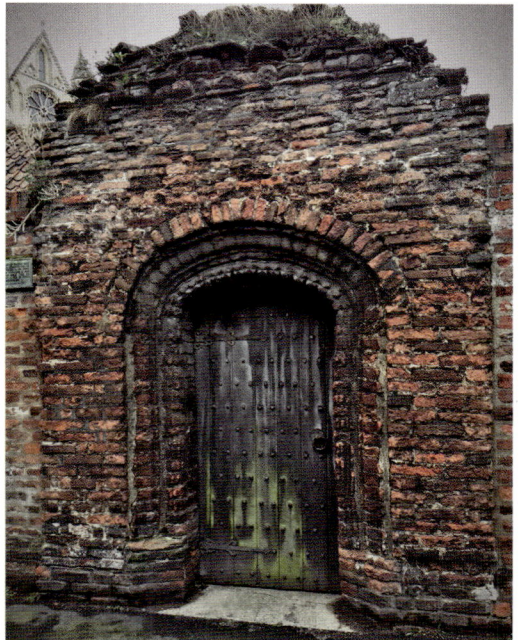

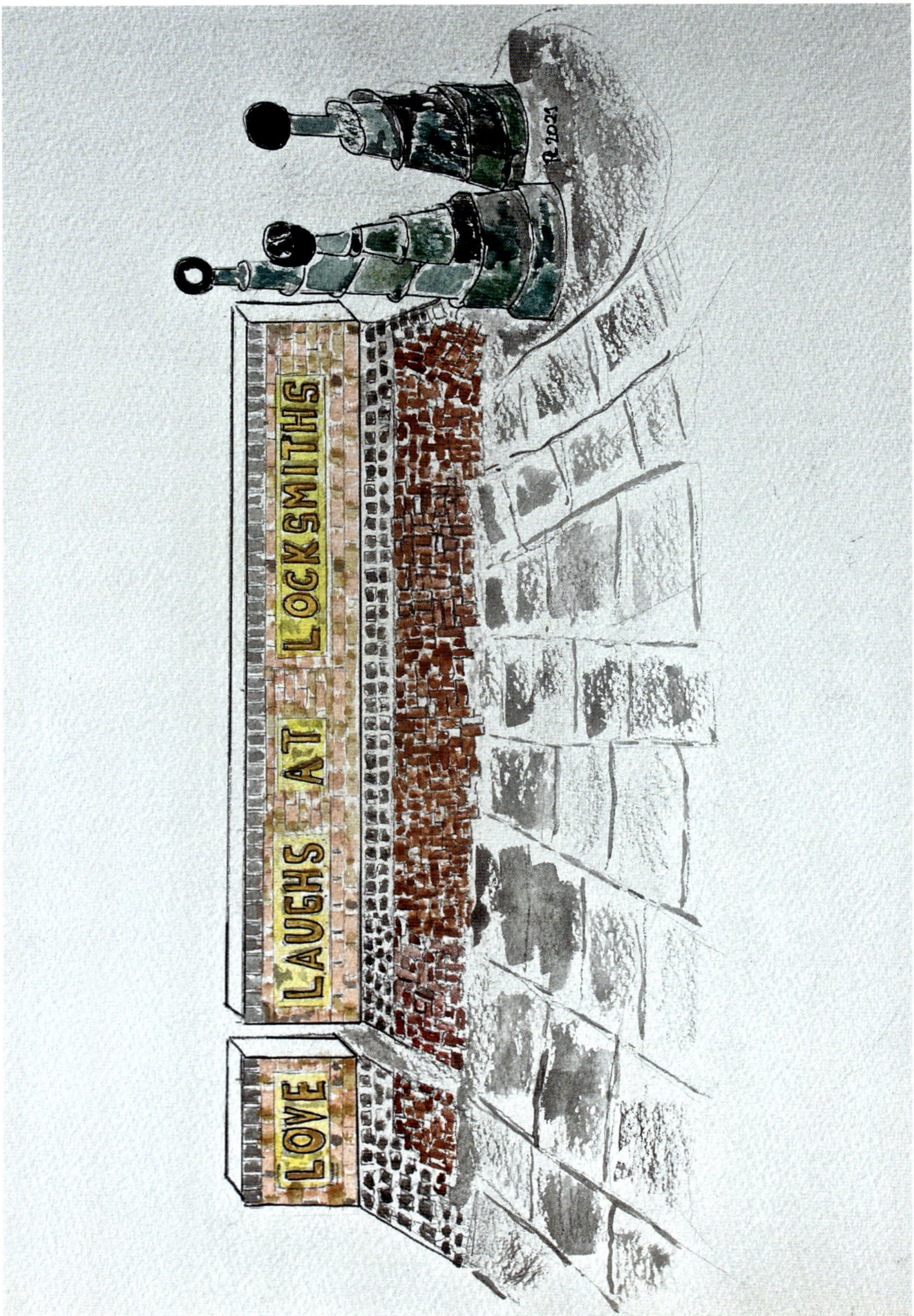
LOVE
LAUGHS AT LOCKSMITHS

AN ODE TO THE SMITHS

The Batsman = The Blocksmith
The Huntsman = The Foxsmith
The Rider = The Jocksmith
The Doctor = The Poxsmith
The Electrician = The Shocksmith
The Herdsman = The Stocksmith

The Watchmaker = The Clocksmith
The Vintner = The Hocksmith
The Postman = The Knocksmith
The Cynic = The Mocksmith
The Singer = The Rocksmith
The Chinese Cook = The Woksmith

THE LOCKSMITHS

It seems likely that in early medieval times the locksmith, as a member of the Guild of Smiths, was the master of many or all of the skills involving metals - including those of the blacksmith, tinsmith, plumber and riveter. However, their own Guild of 'Lockyers' was founded in London in 1422, and no doubt the local Locksmiths' Guilds soon followed.

The earliest locks existed 6,000 years ago and were found in Nineveh, the ancient capital of Assyria. The Egyptians invented simple wooden pin locks which consisted of a bolt, a door attachment and a key with pins that looks like a toothbrush. The Romans were the first to develop metal 'warded' locks, which contained metal projections inside (wards) that the key could only pass through if it was the correct shape. This type of lock was in use throughout the Middle Ages and, although a great deal of time and money was spent in creating ornate locks for monasteries and churches, they were all of the same basic technology. It wasn't until the C18[th] that further developments took place and the first double acting tumbler locks were designed, firstly by Robert Barron and a few years later by Joseph Bramah from Barnsley, whose lock was unpickable for sixty seven years (good, stingy Yorkshireman!!).

In The Town Trail Guide there are pictures of a medieval lock and some of the keys found during excavations in Eastgate - but can you figure out how the lock worked? If not, the diagrams shown opposite may be of help!

The Trail Guide also tells us the words 'Love Laughs at Locksmiths' are the title of a play performed by Beverley Grammar school at the Playhouse Theatre in Lairgate (now demolished). The words are derived from verse in a poem called Venus and Adonis written by William Shakespeare

'Were beauty under twenty locks kept fast
Yet love breaks through, and picks them all at last'.

They are taken to mean that nothing and nobody can keep lovers apart. The C18[th] play using the words as its title was written by George Colman the Younger and first performed at the Little Theatre (or the Theatre Royal) in Haymarket, London in 1803.

So now you know.

PUSH KEY PADLOCK WITH SEPARATE
SPRING SHACKLE

[FROM HISTORICAL LOCKS IN SWEDISH MIDDLE
AGES 1050-1520]

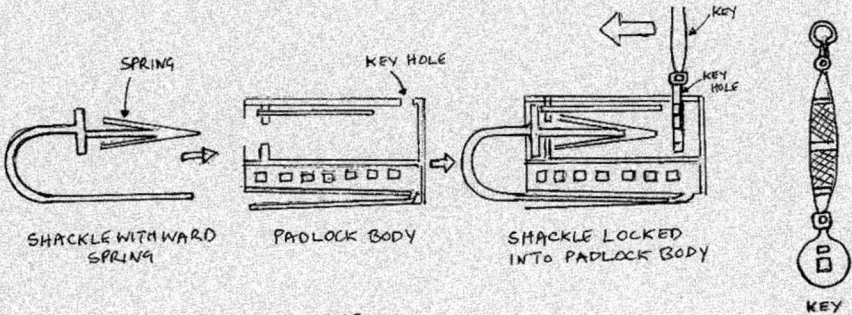

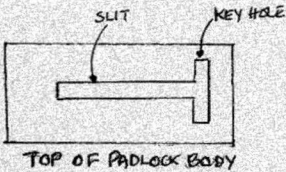

SPRING

KEY HOLE

KEY

KEY
HOLE

SHACKLE WITH WARD
SPRING

PADLOCK BODY

SHACKLE LOCKED
INTO PADLOCK BODY

KEY

SLIT   KEY HOLE

TOP OF PADLOCK BODY

TO OPEN THE LOCK THE KEY IS INSERTED
IN THE KEY HOLE ON TOP OF THE BODY
AND THEN DRAWN THROUGH THE SLIT
WHICH COMPRESSES THE SPRING SO THAT
THE SHACKLE CAN BE WITHDRAWN

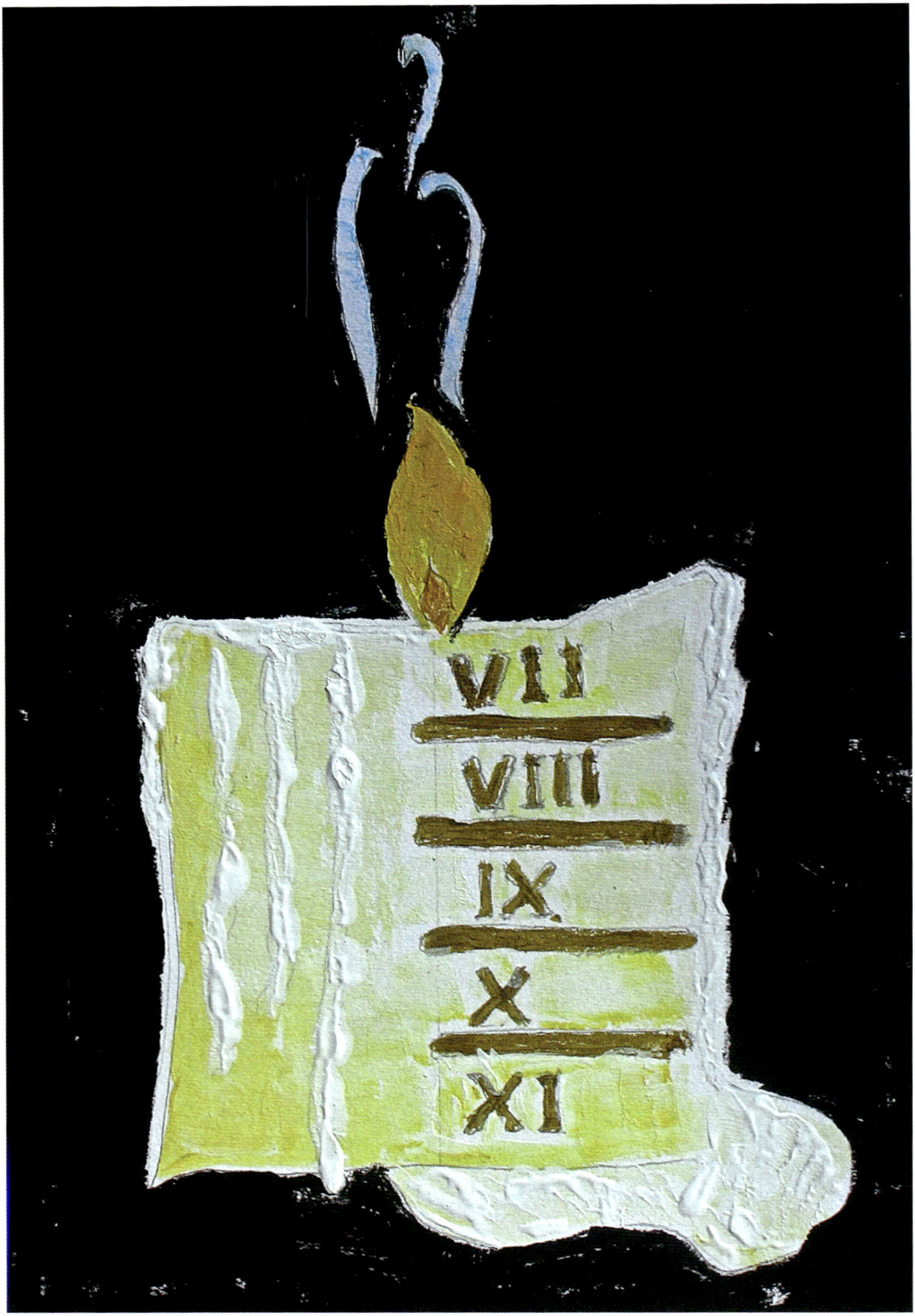
VII
VIII
IX
X
XI

THE CHANDLERS

(*The Candlemakers*)

The chandlers had guilds all over the place,
Key workers in every town.
For candles were always in demand
Each night when the sun went down.

It's not easy for us to quite realise
How people dreaded the night,
When we simply have to touch a switch
And then the room is bright.

So the candlemakers who lived hereabouts
Were fully aware of this:
That they must ensure a ready supply,
An essential East Yorkshire Service.

Ecclesiastical candles were needed as well
Whenever Saints Day rolled in,
And when it came round to their Patron Saint
That Guild was called to dip in.

The Minster, St Mary's, St Nicholas too,
Not forgetting both of the Friaries,
All these churches wanted a few
For the Feast Days they had in their diaries.

THE CHANDLERS

(*The Candlemakers*)

Today we would associate the name 'chandler' with someone who is involved with the nautical business, supplying equipment and parts for boats. In medieval times, however, the chandler was a maker and seller of candles, often dealing in soap and oils as well.

There were two types of chandler - the wax chandler and the tallow chandler. The chandler might make both sorts of candles but by the C13th separate guilds existed for each - the tallow chandler being much inferior. In the Middle Ages candles were the main source of domestic lighting, and this remained the case until the C17th, when oil lighting started to be used.

Tallow candles were the light source of the poor. The tallow was made from the fat of sheep or, if this was not available, fat from deer, cattle and pigs. The fat was chopped into bits and boiled in a large vat to remove the attached muscle and fibrous tissue. The mixture was then pressed to remove the tallow and the remainder (the greaves) was fed to animals. The whole process created an unpleasant 'stink'. The candles were formed by either dipping a wick into the tallow and repeating the process until the requisite size was achieved, or by pouring the tallow into a mould with a wick in its centre. When burned they gave off an unpleasant animal smell, smoked a lot and required constant trimming. A one-pound's weight worth of tallow candles would cost a worker a day's wages.

The History Girls tell us that wax candles were only affordable by the wealthy and the clergy. They were made from beeswax - one honeycomb being required to make a four-inch candle, which made them very expensive. However, they burned slowly without much smoke and with a pleasant smell. The candle wicks were made from twisting reed, linen or flax. It wasn't until the C19th that the much more efficient plaited wick was used.

Now, most importantly, a little more information about the Chandlers' art work which circles the clock tower in front of Beverley station. There are eleven candles set into the cobbles, each burned down by a graded amount. One of these is shown in our painting. These are 'clock' candles, or Overhill's candles, because they are said to have been invented by a candlemaker called Graham Overhill in the C11th. Each candle would have twelve line markings on it. When lit at the top, the candle would burn from line to line at a rate of one hour for each space.

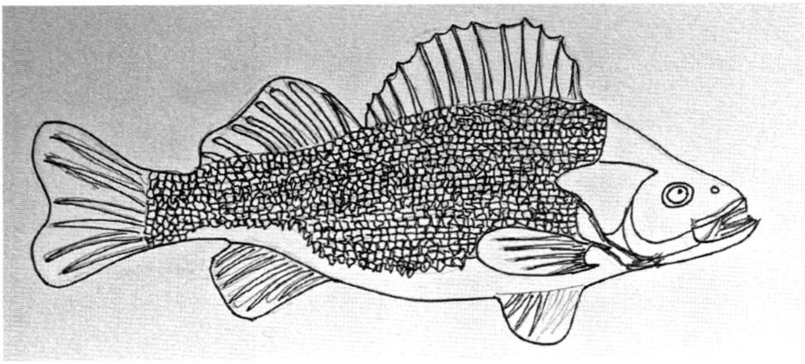

PERCH

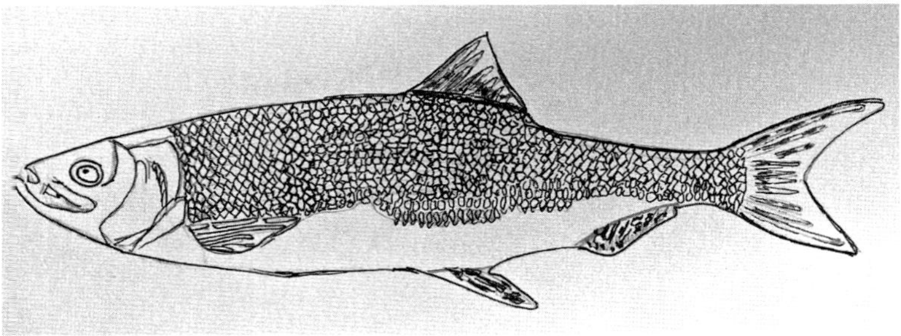

HERRING

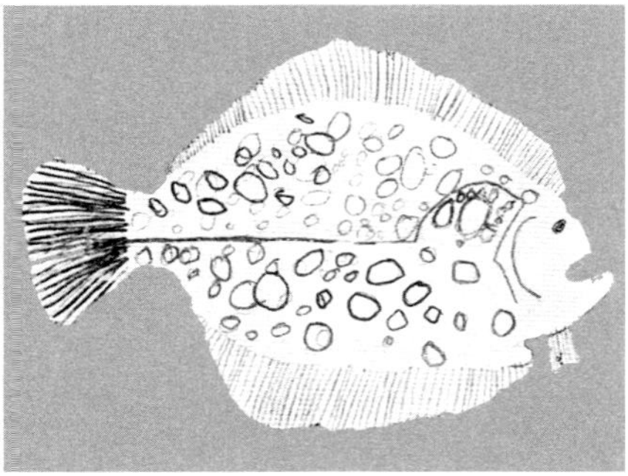

BRILL

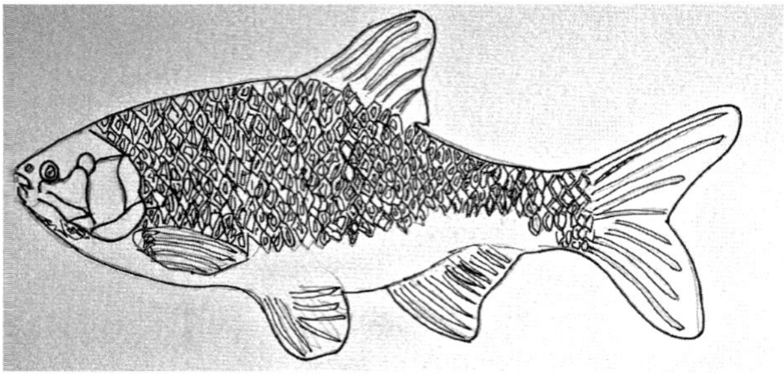

ROACH

74

PERCH

HERRING

BRILL

ROACH

74

THE FISHMONGERS

Fish was an important part of the diet
Of the local population,
And the town authorities had scrutineers
To enforce their regulations.

You weren't allowed to sell stinking fish
No, Sir, not on any account,
Not with an air fresh aerosol,
Not at a huge discount.

Nor were you permitted to sell any fish
That had been out on display,
For slipping fish under the counter, boys,
That wasn't considered fair play.

And just try fishing around midnight
With nets on the Figham Drain,
That would land you the sort of fine
You wouldn't do that again.

The money you received from taxes and fines
Was put to good use, it's supposed,
Safeguarding the archives of the town
And mending the holes in the roads.

Art Installation number 39

THE FISHMONGERS

The fishmonger's shop in Beverley is H. Peck and Sons - we have already featured the shop in *Beverley: Poems, Painting and Prose* (2019). On the paving stones in front of the shop are four engravings - two of freshwater fish (roach and perch), and two of saltwater fish (brill and herring). In medieval times fish was an especially important part of the diet, often being eaten on 'fast' days - of which there were many. Fish were caught in the sea, estuaries, rivers and ponds.

Freshwater fish were caught either in nets, traps or weirs, and sometimes by locals with a rod and line, a spear or a harpoon. A wide variety were sold in the markets - including eel, pike, perch, roach, salmon, trout, bream, rudd, carp and gudgeon. The cheaper fish eaten by the poor were roach, bass and eel. The 'high end' fish eaten by the rich included pike, chub and salmon.

Seawater fish were caught using handheld dip nets or with nets which were lowered over the side of the boat or dragged along the bottom of the seabed. Other methods included the construction of weirs - poles with woven fences between them in a V-shape, which funnelled fish into either nets or fish traps; and bottom fishing with long, baited hooks. Spears and harpoons were also used. In the C14th and C15th the port of Scarborough was important for catching herring, cod and eel. Later on, fish was imported - often from Dutch sources - including salmon, sturgeon, whiting and plaice. The fish was sold either fresh, salted, pickled or smoked. Shellfish were popular, and included oysters, crabs, mussels, scallops and crayfish.

MEDIEVAL FISHING

EEL SPEAR

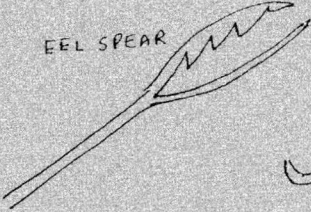

DEAD FISH BAIT

EEL

FISH TRAP

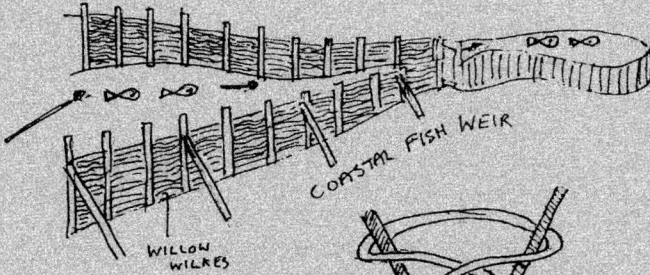

COASTAL FISH WEIR

WILLOW WILKES

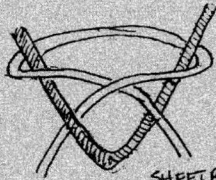

SHEETBEND KNOT

NETTING NEEDLE

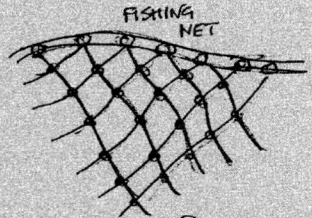

FISHING NET

AFTER SIGLINDESARTS' BLOG
and CLIFFEHISTORY

R 2021

77

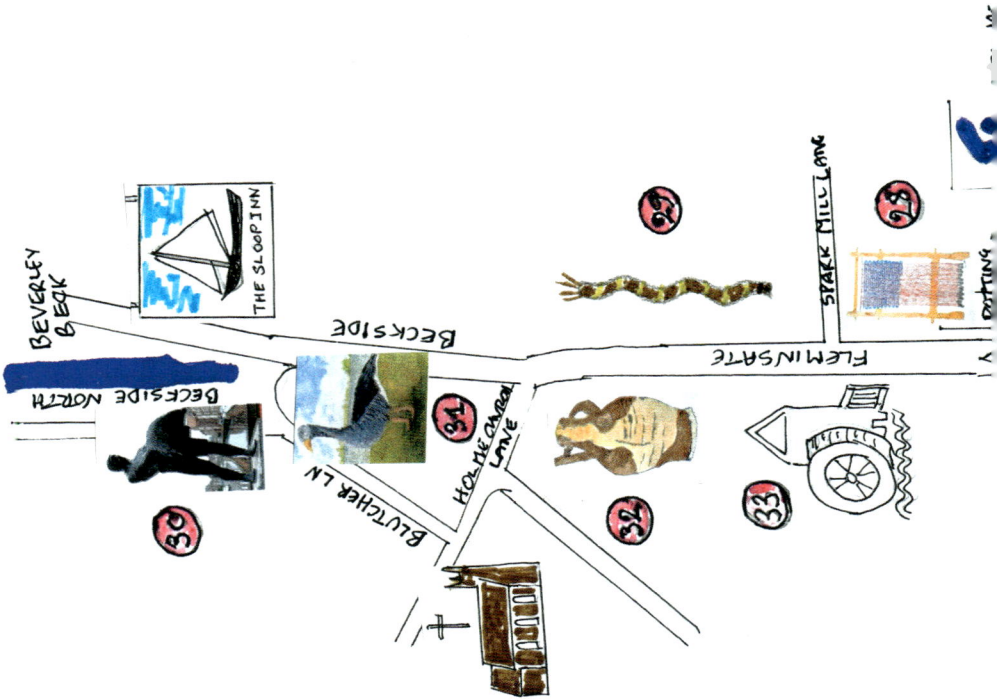

THE SLOOP INN

BEVERLEY BECK

BECKSIDE NORTH

BECKSIDE

BUTCHER LN

HOLME CHURCH LANE

STARK MILL LANE

FLEMINGATE

30

31

32

33

29

23

THE TOWN TRAIL

WALK FOUR

PREMIER INN

FLEMINGATE

FLEMINGATE CENTRE

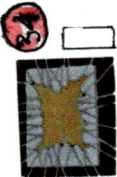

STARBUCKS

ARMSTRONG WAY

FLEMINGATE

FRIARS LANE

LURK LANE

MINSTER RD SOUTH

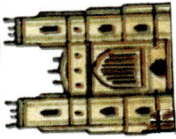

THE MINSTER

EASTGATE

WALK 4

27 SADDLERS

28 WEAVERS

29 ROPE MAKERS

30 CREELERS

31 WILDFOWLERS

32 POTTERS

33 WATER MILLERS

34 TANNERS

35 COOPERS

40 COOKS

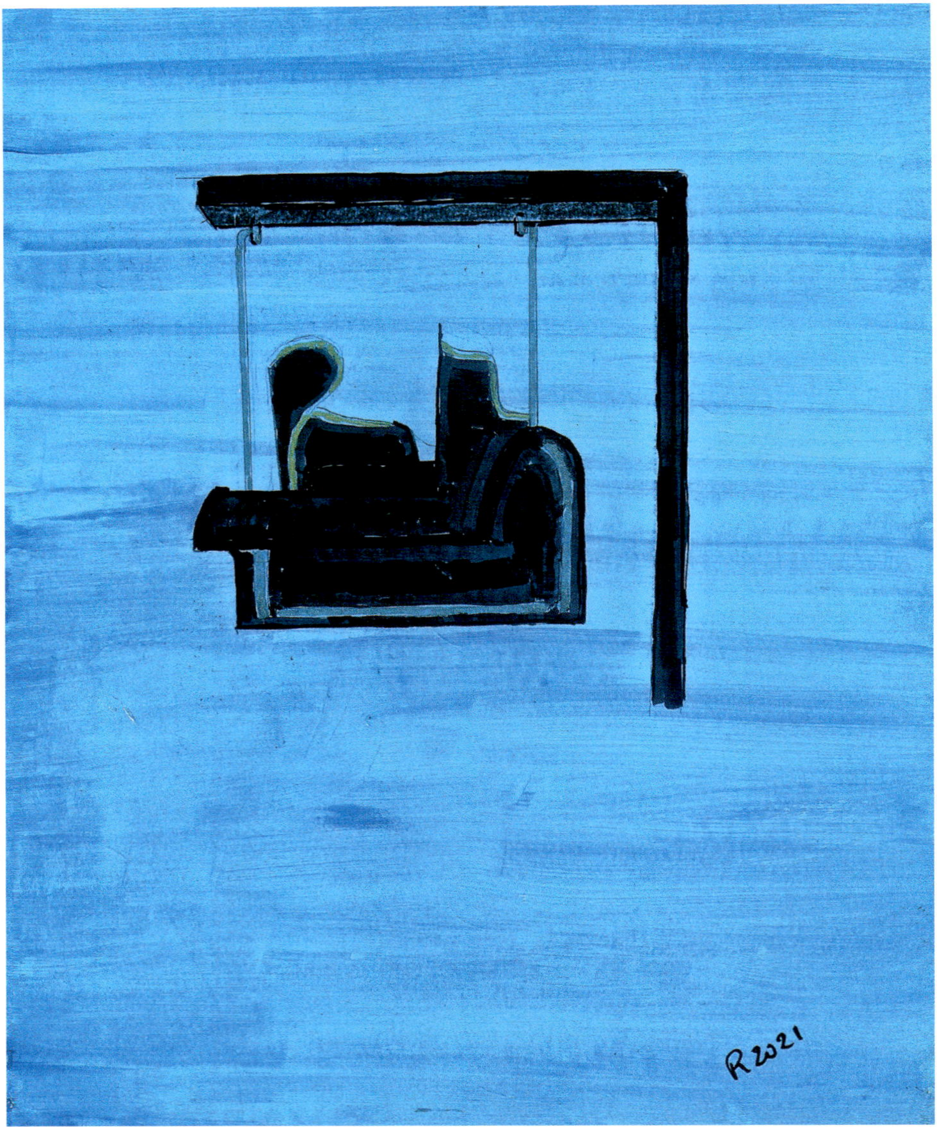
R 2021

THE SADDLERS

Sad to say the saddler does exactly what you'd think:
He stitches saddles all the day, you never see him blink.

The saddles they may range in size, in shape, in style, in leather,
And there cannot be any doubt, the saddler he is clever.

Sheepskin or calfskin he may use for padding on the pommel,
He might have tried out camel skin if he'd worked for Rommel.

The saddle frames he makes of wood, the saddles stuffed with straw,
His customers are always safe, their backsides never sore.

THE SADDLERS

As you walk down Flemingate towards the Beck, on a clear day look up and you will see, on the right-hand side, a medieval saddle suspended from a ' gallows' against the clear blue sky. It looks a funny shape and that is because the medieval saddle used by the knights around the C15th was quite different from the ones used by horse riders today.

The central part of the saddle called 'the tree' was made of linden wood. The solid saddle tree raised the rider above the horse's back and distributed the rider's weight on either side of the animal - thus protecting its spine. At the front, the saddle had a large plate (front cantle, or pommel), also made of wood but sometimes covered with metal. At the back it had a large curved 'cantle' with 'ears' on each side which were hand fashioned to support the rider. The higher cantle and pommel were to help prevent the knight from being unseated in battle.

The saddle was covered in a single layer of linen, sometimes with extra layers of linen on the seat itself. The knight rode with straight legs which were directly against the horse's flanks, where the body of the saddle was cut away. This is a completely different position to the modern-day rider, whose legs are flexed upwards and away from the horse's flanks using 'short stirrups.' The medieval knight's weight was shifted backwards, and only further back were side panels of several layers of linen sometimes stuffed with sheep's wool to provide padding.

In the early Middle Ages the knight often rode without stirrups. In later years long stirrups were used but whether he had them or not the knight prided himself in being able to jump up onto the saddle without a 'leg up.' This was not only a symbol of his fitness but also essential for remounting when he was dismounted during battle. Medieval war horses such as the 'destrier' or great horse, or the lighter, faster 'courses' were not particularly big by modern day standards. They were fit and strong, but one wonders how they coped with the weight of a knight in full armour. The answer is that although the armour looks very heavy in the pictures we see, in fact a full suit of armour weighed between 40-70 pounds (18-32 kg) - which the war horse could carry in his stride - so to speak.

Reconstructed medieval war saddle, circa 1450
(Courtesy Mr Leather)

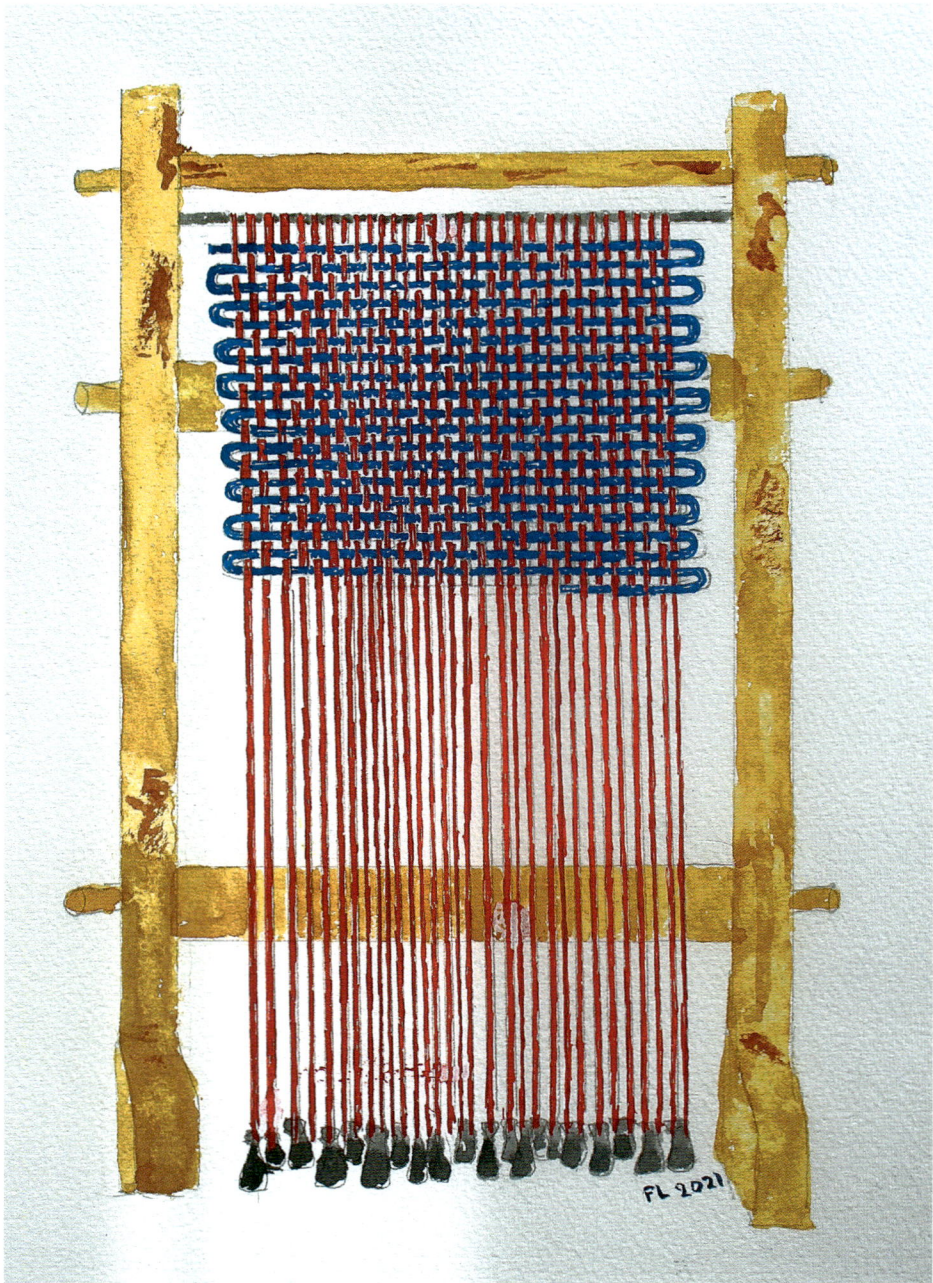

THE WEAVERS

The readers of James Bond books, of whom there must be many,
But I bet there's very few, in fact, if there are any,

Who understand, who comprehend, who do appreciate
The historical importance of our Flemingate.

For here the Flemings came to town and launched
the weaving trade,

And showed us how good lace was spun and how
good bricks were made.

They looked towards the Continent, across the old North Sea,
A journey that was quicker than the road to Withernsea.

They built a thriving export trade to Belgium and beyond -
The authors of prosperity and, of course, James Bond.

THE WEAVERS

In the C13th it is estimated there were fifteen million sheep in England, more than three times the population at that time. Throughout the Middle Ages much of Beverley's affluence was based on the wool and cloth industry. In the C12th-C14th Beverley was a major exporter of raw wool via the port of Hull. The size of the industry is exemplified by records showing that on one occasion in 1313 Beverley merchants chartered three Flemish ships to carry wool worth four thousand pounds - or in today's money worth four million!

The wool exporting trade peaked in 1350 but was succeeded by the growth of the trading and exporting of cloth - an industry which was already well established in Beverley. Indeed, records show royalty purchasing cloth dyed with 'Beverley blues' in the C12th, and the Spanish purchasing 'Beverley scarlets' around the same time.

In 1456 there were four dyers, nine fullers and twenty two weavers in Beverley. Where did all this take place? Well, the weaving and dyeing craftsmen were centred around Eastgate. Merchants from Flanders settled in Flemingate and conducted their weaving and cloth businesses there. The fullers were adjacent to the stream on Walkergate with a plentiful supply of water, and other cloth traders had their shops on the west side of Saturday Market in the area known as The Dings.

The weavers of Beverley produced both functional and beautiful cloth, but it was a multifaceted process as is shown in Appendix 3 'From Sheep's Wool to Cloth'. It has provided us with one or two 'sayings' still in use today: 'dyed in the wool' (no.4 in list) meaning unchanging or inveterate, because when the wool was dyed early its basic colour remained and could not be changed. On tenter hooks (no.10) - sometimes mistakenly written as tender hooks - means 'in a state of suspense'.

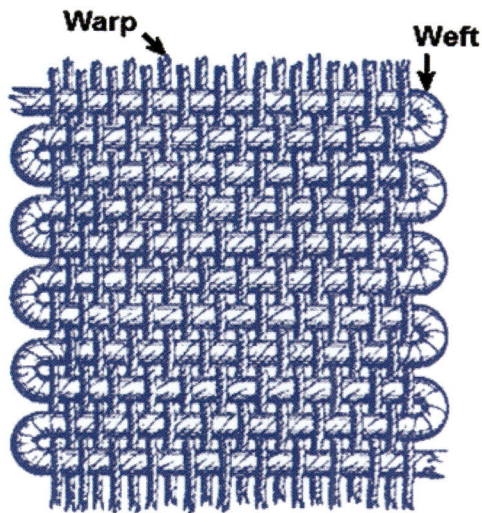

Warp and Weft from Wikipedia:
Medieval Weavers

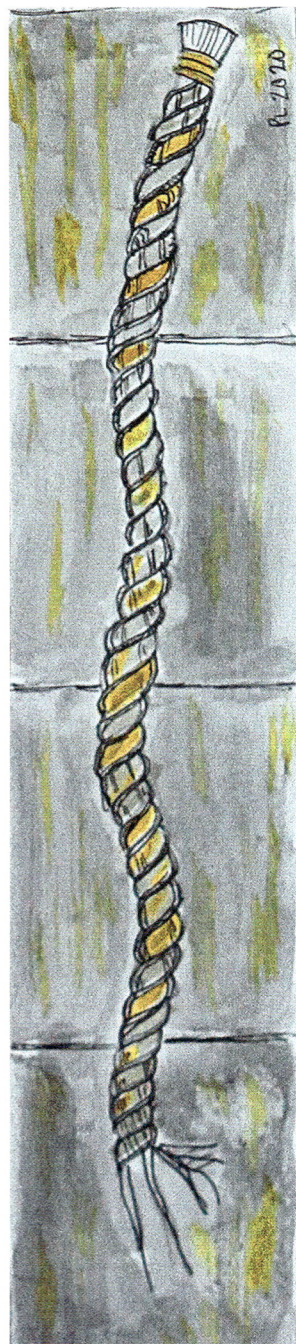

THE ROPEMAKERS

If you listen hard you can hear them talk,
The old ropemakers on the old rope walk -

Walking backwards with a steady tread,
Testing the tension, twisting the thread

For the Pulley Master on the Minster site,
To lift heavy stone to a hazardous height
When lives depended on his rope being right.

More ropes wanted down at the Beck,
To moor all the boats, to keep them in check.

Ropes for the Stockman, the Carter and still
More for the Hangman on Gallows Hill.

THE ROPEMAKERS

Rope making has been part of the lives of humans as long as animals have needed to be led, large stones have been moved around and heavy weights lifted. Pre-historic man used grasses and vines to make ropes, while the Egyptians (3,000 years ago) made rope from the papyrus plant to haul great blocks of stone up the steep sides of the pyramids. In the Middle Ages ropes would be made from reeds and fibres, especially hemp, flax, animal hair and hides for ships. Ropes were an important aspect of the working of great sailing ships as enormous amounts of rope were used for rigging of sails and lowering of anchors. The principle of rope making is the twisting together of six or more yarns to make a strand and then twisting three or four strands together to make a rope.

From the Middle Ages until the coming of factories in the 18th century ropes were constructed in long rope walks where the whole length of the rope could be stretched out and twisted together.

At first a hand spindle was used to twist the yarn but later the construction of rope walks meant that ropes could be stretched out along the length of the walk and ropes could then become longer and stronger. A rope walk was an open path, or an open shed, along which men walked backwards whilst playing out rope fibres from a supply carried round their waists. A rotating hook would twist strands of fibres (made from hemp or similar fibres) together to make a rope. The rope held together because the twists went in opposite directions.

In Beverley the remains of a ropewalk can be seen in the pathway leading from Woodlands to Westwood. Twine, yarn and ropes could also be spun and twisted in the long gardens behind the houses in the town and hung out in the streets.

Throughout the medieval period rope was used in the construction of magnificent cathedrals and churches. Over the two hundred years in which Beverley Minster was built the technology of building developed. More powerful cranes and stronger ropes meant that larger blocks of stone could be used when building the nave. Over the past one hundred years the range of materials used have been altered and now include mineral origin (nylon and polyester) which is lighter to carry and stronger. Here ropes are twisted and formed by machine into even greater length.

In June 2021 a demonstration of the advantage of ropes was the re-painting of the clockface in the West Tower of Beverley Minster. Craftsmen, in order to save on erecting scaffolding, were lowered by rope from the top of the tower to reach the clock and re-gild with 25 carat gold the numbers and hands of the clock.

Medieval Ropemaker (Mendel c 1425) WikiCC share alike

THE CREELER

The Creeler stands beside the Beck,
A fine athletic figure.
Carrying a hefty sack
With strength and ease and vigour.

How quiet now the old Beckside,
How still the placid water.
No sign of old commercial craft,
No employment for the porter.

But here was once an inland quay,
Where laden boats discharged
The bricks, the wood, the peat, the stone,
As Beverley Town enlarged.

Now not a single creel in sight,
Borne on a burly shoulder.
But ghosts appearing in the night,
As memories grow colder.

THE CREELER

The Creeler stands tall at the head of Beverley Beck, a life-size bronze statue of the medieval porter who unloaded the ships and barges in days gone by. I believe he is by far and away the most expensive of the Trail artworks - a fitting tribute to the port of Beverley in medieval times. It is easy to forget that in the C13th Beverley was the tenth largest town in England and a major importer and exporter of goods via the Beck and the River Hull. What was Beckside like in those days? I can do no better than quote from The Beverley Beck Heritage Walk: "Boats laden with stone for the new Beverley Minster arrive at the wharf. Others are loaded with wool destined for Holland and Belgium. Creelers, or carriers, unload heavy baskets (creels) full of firewood or barrels of milk or salt, while carters and porters wait with barrows and sleds to carry the goods into town. The air is ringing with the sound of deals being struck in the market between the two bridges, and the air thick with smoke from the brick and tile yards that line the beck and the stink of the nearby tanneries''. Think of this as you stand in the relative peace and quiet of today's renovated Beckside - with its elegant new houses, dredged and cleaned waterway, the footpaths and cycle routes and the beautifully restored old barges. And let's give a vote of thanks to the Archbishop of York, Thurstan, who in the C12th had the foresight to clear the River Hull of the fish nets and open up the waterway to Beverley.

ML 2021

GREYLAG

THE WILDFOWLERS

In just two words you can explain
How our world has changed,
How we cope with excess rain,
How things are rearranged.
FLOOD PLAIN

When February used to fill the dykes
When rivers burst their banks,
Huge areas of overflow
'longside the river banks.
FLOOD PLAIN

Where once sweet water meadows lay
Ranks of sad houses stand,
And rescue teams pump out all day
The underwater land.
FLOOD PLAIN

And where's the fowler's shallow boat,
And where's his outspread net?
And where's the flocks of geese and ducks?
We're waiting for them yet.
FLOOD PLAIN

THE WILDFOWLERS

In medieval times the peat marshes of the Hull Valley, beside which Beverley stands, were subject to regular flooding and served as a breeding ground for fish and wildfowl. This was the hunting ground for the wildfowler (or wetfowler). Many diverse types of bird would be found there, including little grebe, teal, duck, wild goose, mallard, snipe, heron and swan. Gunpowder was not widely available until the C18th so the medieval wildfowler used other methods to catch his prey - spears, bows and arrows, nets and nooses, snares, decoys, baits and poisons. He even trained dogs to act like foxes and splash in the water to attract gregarious ducks (in The Netherlands: the *KookerHondje).*

I just love the sculpture of the 'greylag goose' which stands on Blucher Lane at its junction with Beckside - though I am told the regulars of the adjacent taverns were less pleased when it was installed: "We're stuck with a mucky goose whilst posh folk up west get all the nice things". The sculpture raises an interesting point: the goose is depicted upright with an exceedingly long neck and little colouring - more like the domestic white Emden goose than the wild greylag Anser anser, which has a shorter neck and horizontal body as shown in Mary Laycock's beautiful painting. I'm sure the ornithologists will put us right.

It should be remembered that game birds were an important part of the diet, especially of the wealthy. I have seen it stated that in C18th London the estimated yearly consumption of geese was 26,000, the same number of turkeys per year and 2,000 capers, 500 dozen chickens, 4,300 ducks and 2,000 pigeons per week over an eight month period.

Incidentally turkeys were introduced to the UK by a sailor, William Strickland, in the late C15th - he lived in Boynton Manor, near Bridlington.

Lastly a short word about the swan. The swan was a regular feature of many a medieval banquet, often as the centre piece or 'a subleties' with the swan roasted, skinned and redressed in all its glory - or maybe stuffed with a series of increasingly smaller birds (turducken). I have never eaten swan but those who have seem varied in their assessment - some say it tastes 'fishy', halfway between beef and pork and more like chicken than duck. It would appear that most of the swans in England are free and do not belong to anyone - The Queen owns only the mute swans on the Thames. The only people today who are allowed to eat swans are 'The Royals', and The Fellows of St John's College, Cambridge on June 25th - neither group exercises its right, so leave them alone !

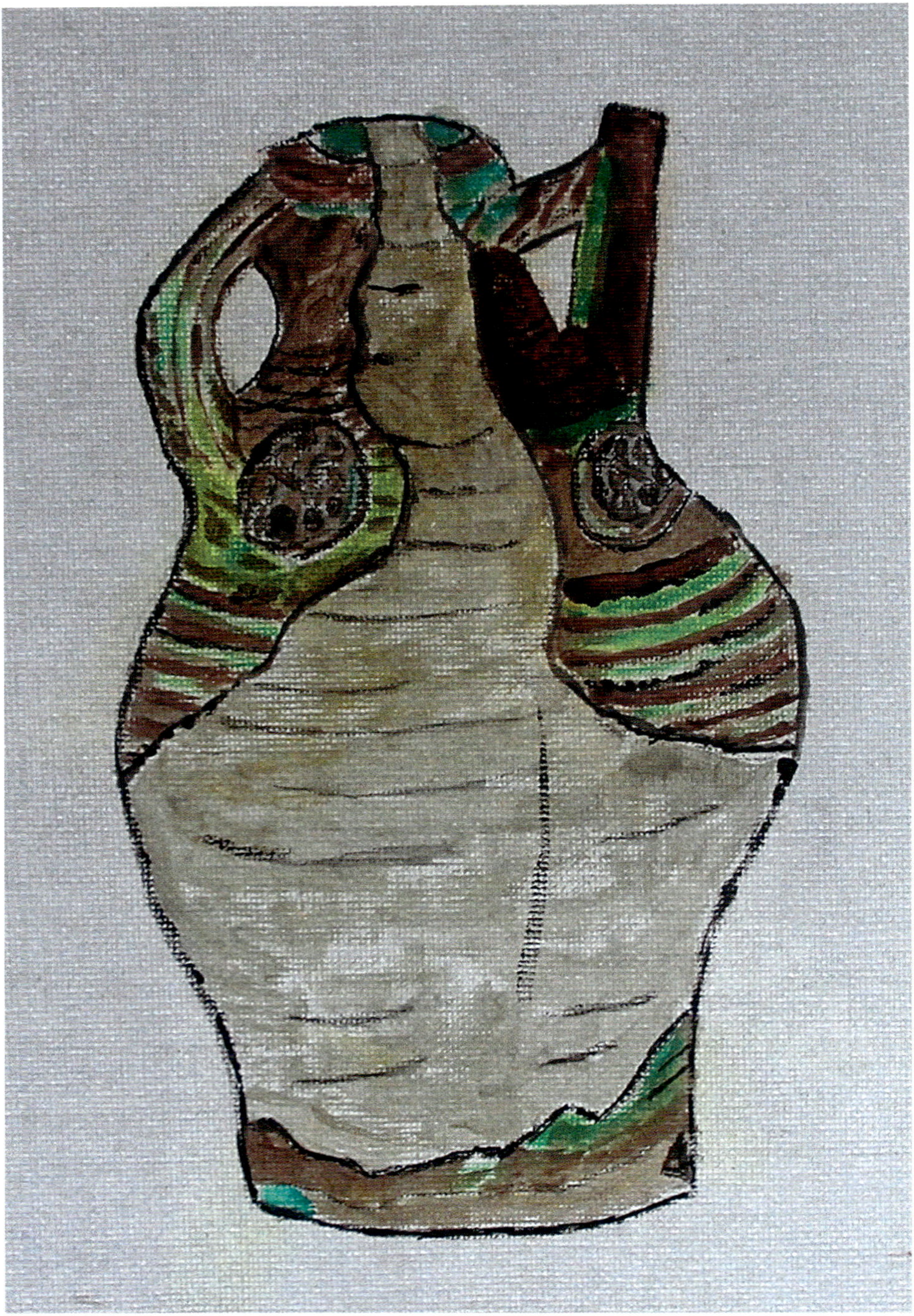

THE POTTERS

The Beverley Potters were pretty well placed
Having good boulder clay close at hand
In a prosperous town which had certainly grown
Where their product was much in demand.

Their earliest type of utility pots
Were plain, with a splash of green glaze.
This seemed rather crude as their techniques improved
And they sought more decorative ways.

Then came the Black Death and the town held its breath,
Who would survive, who would not?
It was in those dark days they coined the catch phrase:
'The world is going to pot'.

But those who survived, their skills still alive,
Produced glorious glazed earthenware -
Strong green, purple-brown, it was very well known
And branded as fine Humberware.

THE POTTERS

In early medieval times pottery tended to be a rural pursuit as there was an adjacent source of clay and sand, wood for the kiln and plenty of water. Later on, the potters moved into the towns. In Beverley, by the C12th the centre of the industry was in Grovehill ('Grevale'), where there was plenty of clay and, after construction of the Beck, a nearby means of export. There are three main types of pottery, namely earthenware, stoneware and porcelain. These involve specific types of clay heated to different temperatures. In early days mainly earthenware was created, crafted by hand, as the pottery wheel did not come in until much later.

The Humber Archaeology Partnership tells us that the potteries created were called Beverley wares. Those produced in the C12th and C13th are now called Beverley 1 wares, and consisted of jugs, cooking pots, curfews (large bowls that were turned upside down over the embers of the fire at night) and pipkins (small, handled cooking pots), all covered in lead glazes by splash glazing. Because the local clays contained iron oxide, the fired pottery had a reddish tinge - hence the term 'orangeware'. In the late C13th and C14th higher quality products were made, and these are now known as Beverley 2 wares. A much wider variety of vessels were made using more carefully prepared clay, and the glazing was performed by dipping the vessels (called suspension glazing).

By the way, pottery and ceramics are really one and the same. The word ceramic is derived from the Greek *keramicos*, which means pottery. Both pottery and ceramics describe objects which have been formed with clay and hardened by firing. The purist would say that **pottery** is a specific form of **ceramics** using clay; and that **ceramics** can involve a similar use of other materials such as tile, glaze, zirconium oxide and silica.

I knew you would want to know that.

Beverley 1 ware
(Painting after an exhibit in Yorkshire Museum)

The Water Millers by Stephen Hill

THE WATER MILLERS

The image of the water mill beside a country steam
In a pre-industrial age, a Constable-like scene.

In truth it very frequently was of another kind,
A miller's life has been described as one long bloody grind.

For windmillers it weren't so bad, for if the wind weren't blowing
They often had the whole day off, without the bosses knowing.

For water millers no such luck, for water keeps on flowing -
It's noses to the grindstone lads, there's nowhere you are going.

THE WATER MILLERS

The Domesday book of 1085 mentions 3 mills in Beverley i.e. mills driven by water (this gives an indication of the size of Beverley at that time for 3 mills would produce enough flour for about 3,000 people). The Archbishop of York, being the Lord of the Manor of Beverley, owned the land on which the mills were placed near the Beck. His agent, or reeve, took a proportion of the profits, named a Mill Soke. Throughout the medieval period the water miller would be provided with the main timbers and millstones for the mill, the tenant being responsible for the rest of the timber.

Water mills are also mentioned in the Town documents in 14th/15th and 16th centuries. Throughout the medieval period members of the Water Millers Guild would be expected (if they could afford it) to wear the livery of the guild when attending feasts or processions. The livery consisted of a long robe, or a short robe for younger members. During the feast of Corpus Christi, in early June, the mystery plays would be performed throughout the town. The play performed by the Water Millers was the Raising of Lazarus. Guildsmen were expected to learn their lines, and their costumes and props had to be in order for the 'honour of the community'. The wagon on which the play was performed was decorated with bedspreads as a backcloth. During the medieval period there is no mention of windmills on Westwood presumably because of the large number of trees which were there. In 1625 there was a lawsuit in which a tenant of the Water Mill complained that the windmills on Westwood were taking away their trade. Apparently, Water Millers were struggling to provide sufficient flour for the needs of the townspeople and also for tenants at Thearne, Weel and Woodmansey. Bowing to the inevitable, one Water Miller erected a windmill close by the water mills.

Water mills were still working in the town in 1749 in tandem with new technology which included horse mills which needed neither water nor wind to grind corn.

Water Mill Luttrell-Psalter Br. Library

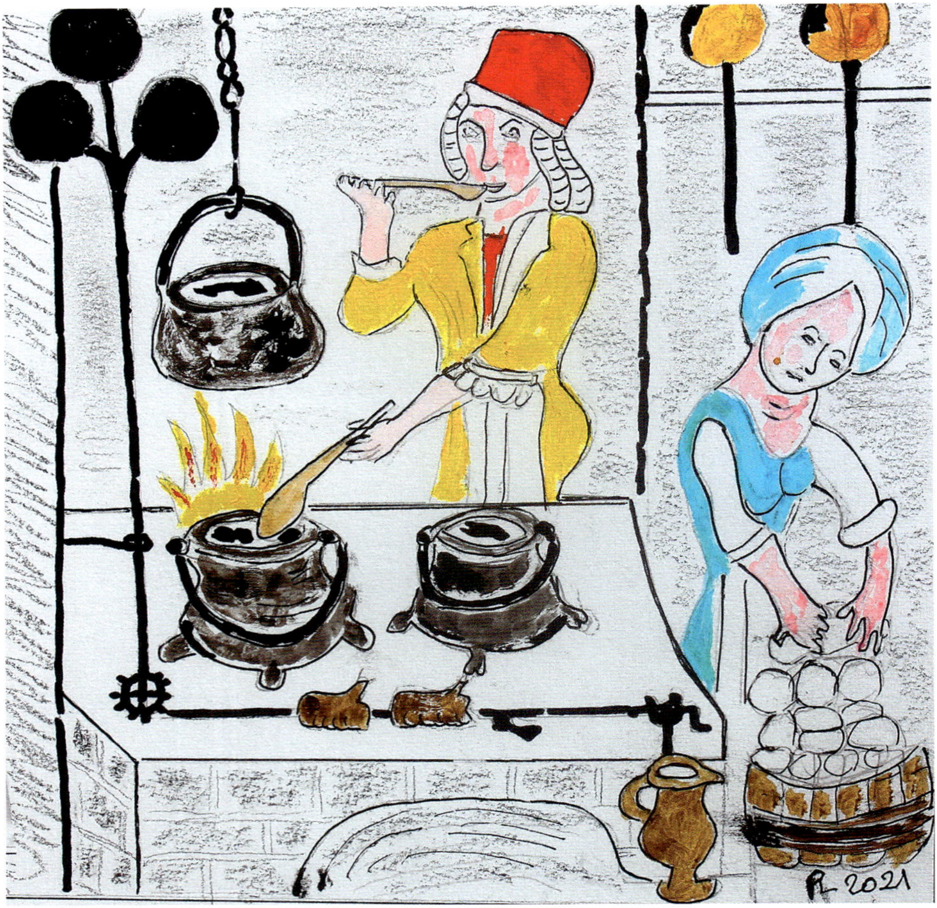

THE COOKS

The medieval kitchen…that was the meeting place
of two quite different cultures, of language and of race.

The Cook was Anglo-Saxon, the Chef - mais oui - was French,
The Chef was married to Madame, the Cook had wed the Wench.

The Cook would dish up English lamb, the Chef served only mutton,
The Chef was out to please the palate, the Cook to please the glutton.

The food was cooked upon the hearth with wood and charcoal lit,
The meat was tossed into the pot, the game turned on the spit.

Mealtime was a boozy job, the guests served at the table,
The villeins sat where'er they could and grabbed what they were able.

THE COOKS

The painting on page 108 shows a cook at the hearth with her trademark ladle and is taken from a woodcarving published in *Kuchenmaistrey* - a German cookery book first published in 1485. In the large houses and castles of the medieval days the cooking was done on a big hearth which was in the centre of the room with the fires of wood and charcoal lit on top of the hearth as shown. The heat also served to warm the room, but the smoke and fumes floated up to a hole in the ceiling. It wasn't until later that the stoves were moved to a back wall and equipped with a chimney. The interesting 'clover leaf' apparatus on the left is a windmill, driven by the fire eddies and currents turning the spit, on which game can be seen roasting. I think the 'sous-chef' is preparing further birds for the spit. The common foods eaten were meat - game in the form of chicken, goose and duck, and also quail, partridge and songbird; pork, beef, but not much as cattle were expensive to breed and feed. Fish was common - herring, salmon, eel and trout as well as shellfish - oyster, crab and mussels. Bread was eaten a lot - only the wealthy could afford fine white flour, so the poorer people ate dark, coarse bread. Fruit, either fresh, dried or preserved was popular and, for the well off, there were puddings such as fritters, crepes, custards and tarts served with cheeses and copious wine and mead.

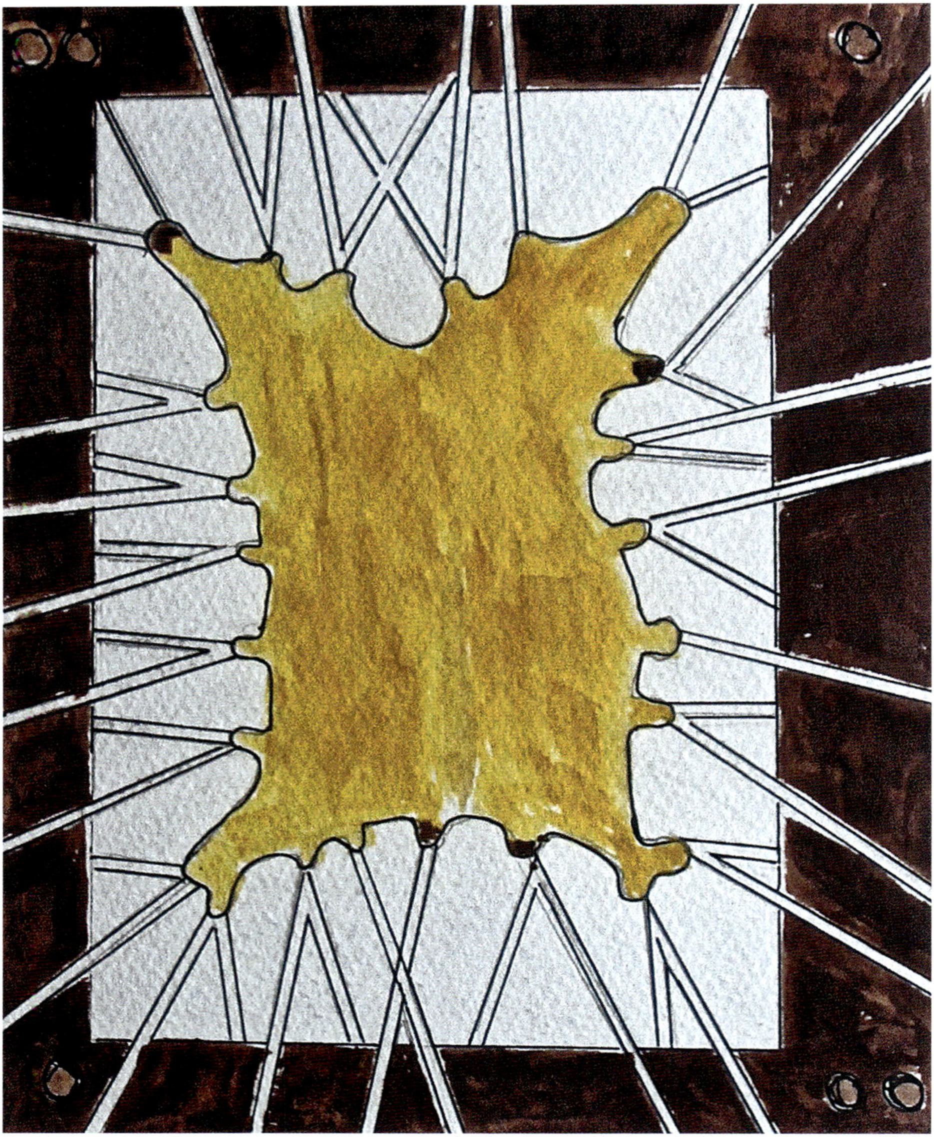

THE TANNERS

Beverley was always a tannery town
Right back in the dark Middle Ages,
A very important financial support
Providing employment and wages.

But after the War, the world it had changed,
As cheap imports flooded in
And new synthetic materials were used,
And the tanneries' profits grew thin.

The trainer had hit the leather shoe trade
And fashion became more informal,
And cobblers ran out of shoes to repair
And the 'throw it away' became the normal.

Then Hodgson's and Melrose Tanneries closed
With many a tear and a sigh
To be replaced by the caravan
And the likes of ABI.

THE TANNERS

After the wool and cloth industry, tanning was the next most important trade in medieval Beverley. This was because Beverley had excellent access to the prerequisites - namely sheep and other animals for their skins, oak trees for the natural tannins in their bark, chalk pits for the lime, and plenty of water for the many steps involved in leather production.

The tanners of Beverley produced the high quality leather demanded by the cordwainers, jerkin makers, armourers, glovers, saddlers and their demanding customers. The leather produced was called 'vegetable tanned' leather because the tannins used were from natural sources - that is trees or plants. After 1850 much leather was tanned with chrome salts and would be termed 'chromed leather'. The process of tanning causes both chemical and physical changes in the raw animal skin, making it durable, flexible and both water and stain resistant.

The entire process might involve many people – **the skinners** to flay the animals, and **the fellmongers** to remove the fat and hair (a dirty, smelly process involving applications of bird droppings, urine and dog dung!) and to sell the skins to the tanners. Then there were t**he barkers** who prepared the oak tree bark, **the tanners** themselves and finally **the curriers,** who finished or dressed the leather by stretching, pressing and sometimes dyeing it.

The tanning process itself is worthy of a little more attention. Two pits were involved. In the first, the prepared hide was repeatedly dipped in a weak solution of bark tannin until the required colour was obtained. In the second pit, the hides were layered with oak bark and a solution of tannin or cold water poured over them and then left for anything up to a year before finally being handed over to the currier for finishing.

The Beverley Tanners' Guild was formed in 1337 and by 1366 there were thirty tanners working in the town (out of a population of five thousand!). Because the tanneries were classed as a noxious or 'odoriferous' industry, they tended to be pushed to the edges of the town. Evidence of tan pits and bark residue has been found in Keldgate, Lurk Lane, Champney Road and Flemingate amongst other places. Remember all this next time you pull on your lovely soft leather shoes or gloves, and if you want to know more look at the pdf of the brilliant exhibition put on by East Yorkshire Museums.

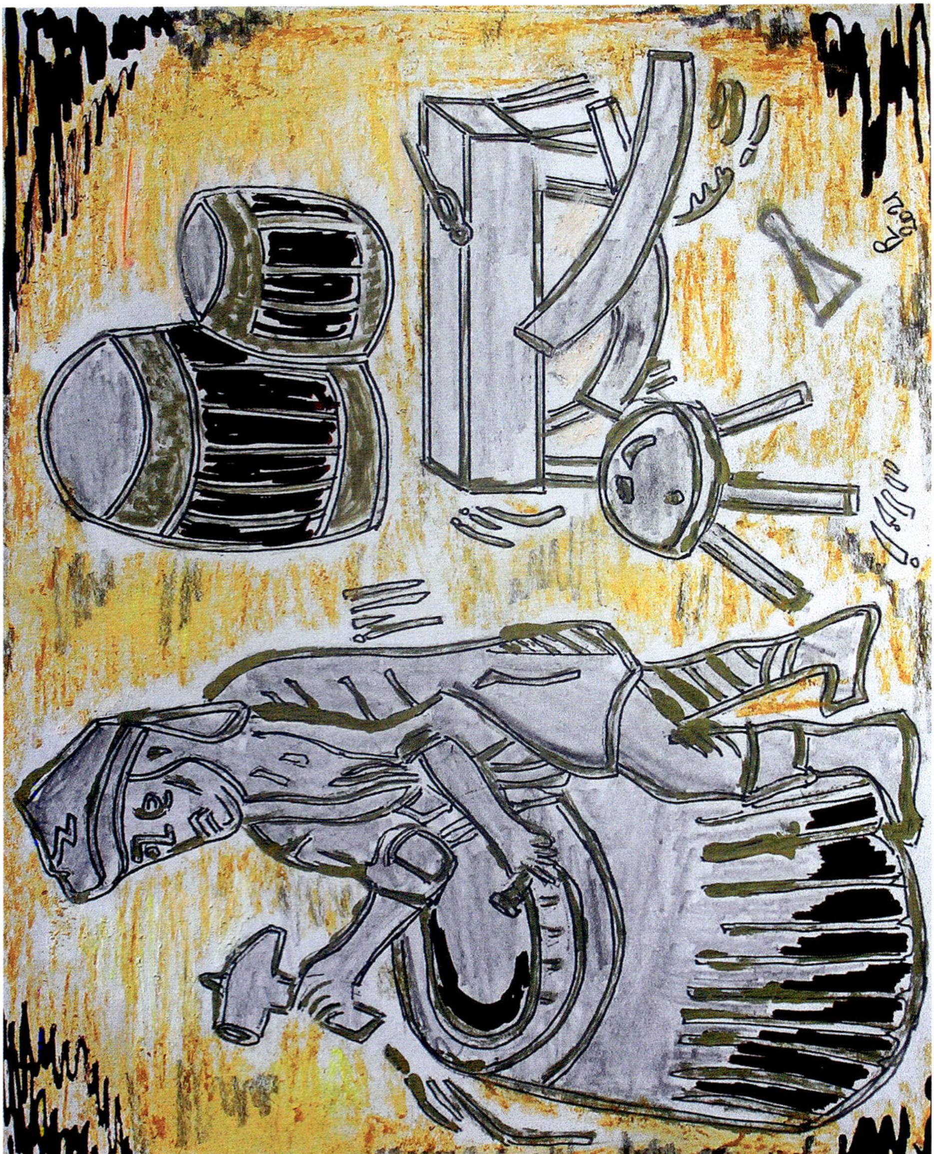

THE COOPERS

The coopers made containers, containers made of wood,
They used their ingenuity, they made them pretty good.

If you had liquids to be stored or else to be transported,
At prices that you could afford, the cooper'd get it sorted.

The barrels and the water carts, the pails, the casks, the tubs,
They made them for the tradesmen and the landlords of the pubs.

The woods they used were English oak and English beech and lime,
Left to season in their yards, or sometimes soaked in brine.

The staves were planed and carefully shaped, so when bound together
They were completely watertight, 'twas really very clever.

Those were craftsmen, no mistake, and what was so fantastic,
If you wandered round their works you'd find NO bloody plastic!!

THE COOPERS

A medieval cooper was someone who made wooden casks, barrels, vats, tubs and troughs. Cooper is derived from the Middle Dutch *cuper*, or cask, and the Latin *cupa*, or barrel. The barrels he made had different names depending on how much they would hold: hogsheads, tuns, firkins, tierces, rundlets and puncheons. In medieval times he was a very important and busy craftsman, as his vessels were much in demand for storage (beer, wine, food - including salted beef), buckets for carrying water or milk, churns for cheese and milk, tubs for food storage and even bigger vessels for fulling cloth, dyeing, tanning and bathing. The cooper also made drinking vessels - many of them ornate and valuable. His assistant - the journeyman - made wooden implements such as rakes and shovels to supplement his income. Apparently there were four divisions of the coopers' crafts: **dry coopers,** who made vessels for shipping dry goods; **dry tight coopers,** who made vessels which kept goods dry and moisture out (e.g. for gunpowder); **white coopers,** who made straight staved containers which were watertight though not made for the purpose of shipping (e.g. bath tubs); and finally the **wet or tight coopers,** who made watertight barrels for shipping or transporting (beer or wine for example).

The latter barrels involved bending the wood and thus required more skill, time and cost. The coopers' tools were quite simple - mallets, axes and shaving tools. The wood of choice was oak. In the early Middle Ages the straight staved container had wooden bands to hold the staves together but, as the iron industry developed, metal hoops became the bands of choice and the 'hooper' became a craftsman in his own right. The craftsman cooper is a rare person nowadays. If you have a little time to spare listen on YouTube to the Australian George Smethwick describe his life as a traditional cooper - worth it if only for his tale at the end about how his dad made his bourbon whisky!

Preparando una Barrica
(Wiki: GNU Free Licence)

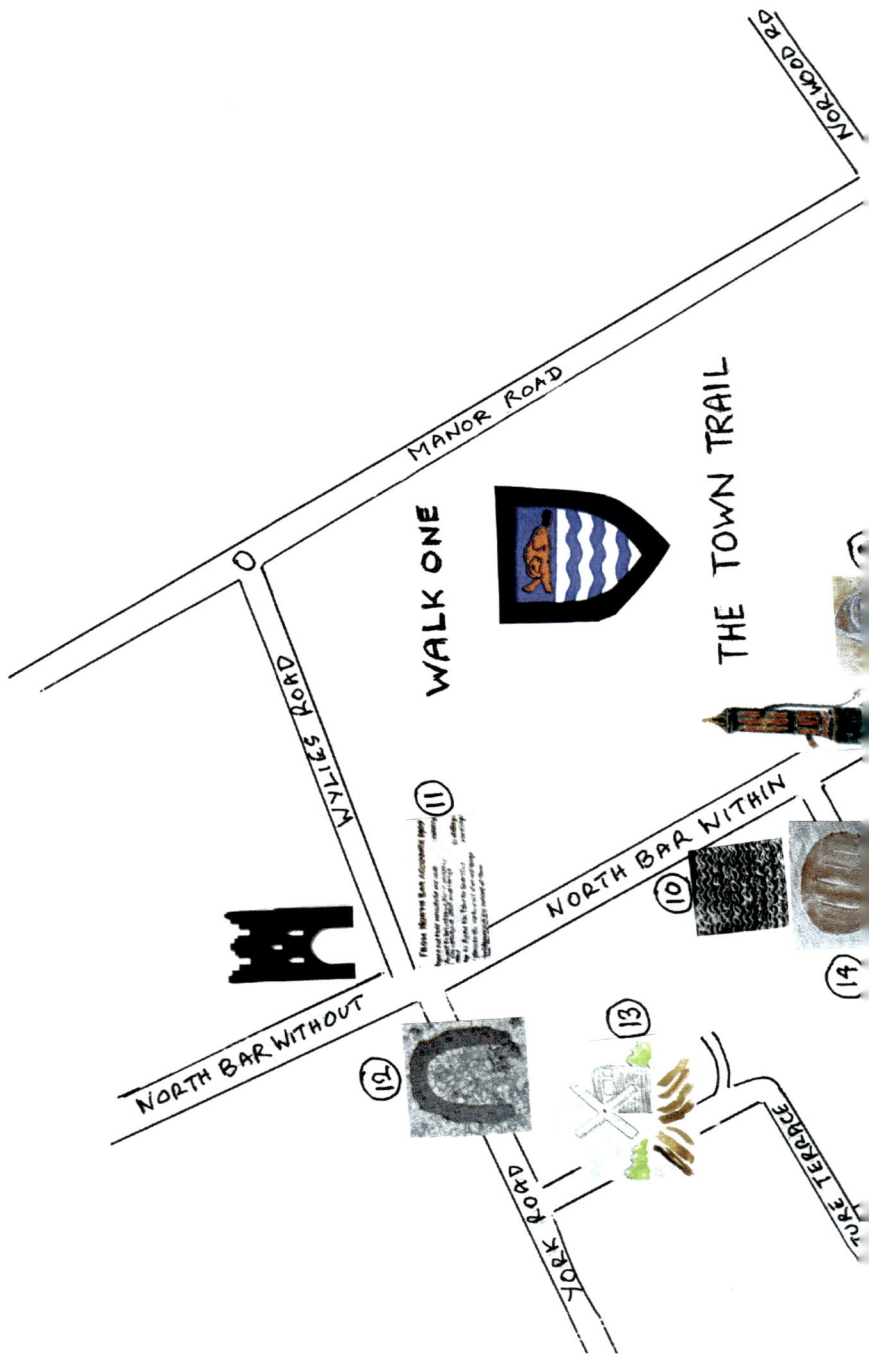

NORWOOD RD

MANOR ROAD

WALK ONE

THE TOWN TRAIL

WYLIES ROAD

NORTH BAR WITHIN

⑪

Please observe & use accompanying type.

⑩

NORTH BAR WITHOUT

⑫

⑬

⑭

YORK ROAD

TURE TERRACE

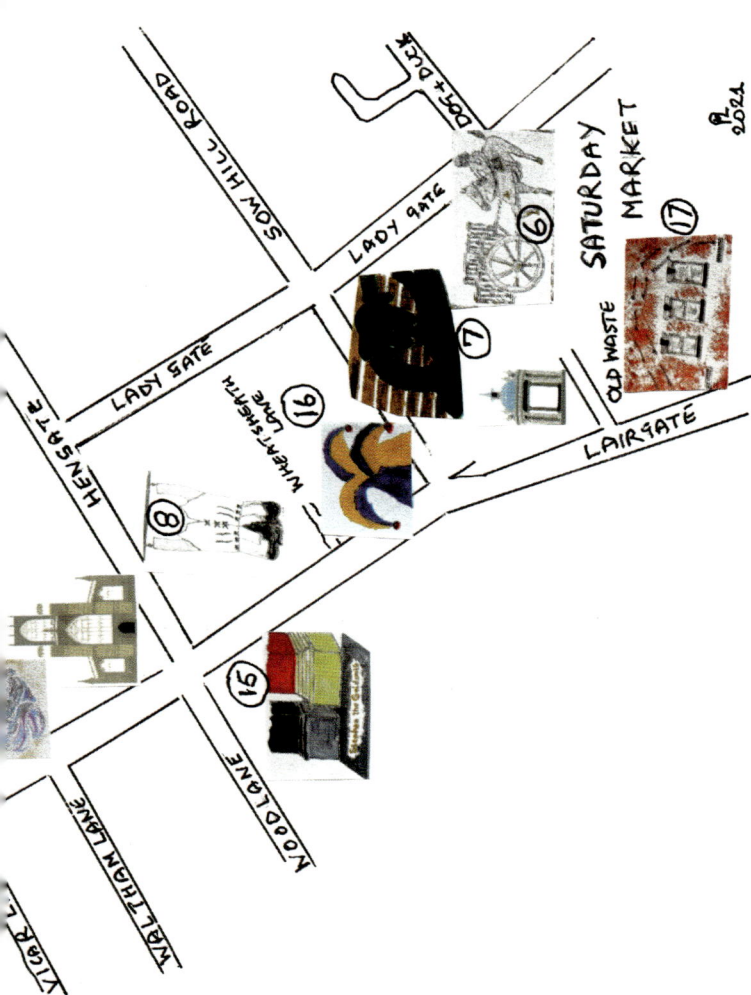

Map labels:
- VICAR L... (top left area)
- TIGER ...
- WALTHAM LANE
- SOW HILL ROAD
- LADY GATE
- LADY GATE
- DOG + DUCK
- HENGATE
- WHEATSHILL LANE
- NOODLANE
- LAIRGATE
- OLD WASTE
- SATURDAY MARKET
- ⑥
- ⑦
- ⑧
- ⑯
- ⑮
- ⑰

R
2021

WALK 1

6 CARTMEN
7 GLOVERS
8 JERKIN MAKERS
9 MINSTRELS
10 ARMOURERS
11 BRICKLAYERS
12 FARRIERS
13 WINDMILLERS
14 BAKERS
15 GOLDSMITHS
16 HATTERS
17 FLETCHERS

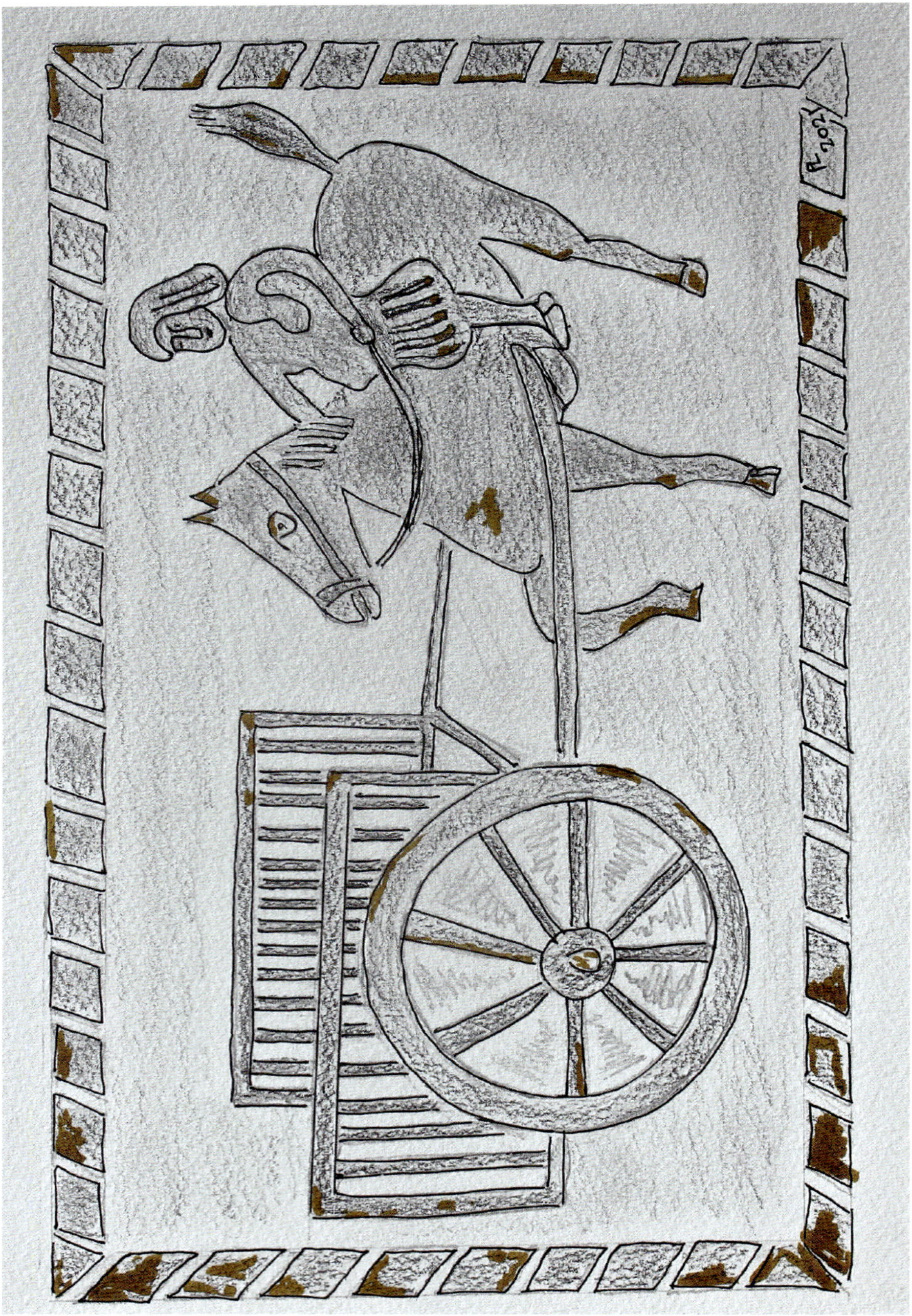

THE CARTMEN

The cartmen were the go-to-guys when you had heavy loads
That needed to be shifted on the dodgy roads.
They swore and coaxed the carthorse who had to pull his weight,
For which they were rewarded at a miserly sort of rate.

There were no unions at that time, and so they formed a Guild
To negotiate on their behalf, and they were duly thrilled
When they agreed a standard fee from Beckside into Town
Of half a pence per horse load - you could have knocked
'em down.

Horse and Cart Misericord and its Supporters (permission Beverley Minster)

THE CARTMEN

The art installation dedicated to the Cartmen of Beverley is a bronze plaque depicting a horse and cart with the cart placed before the horse! It is quite difficult to find but lies on a paver in front of the newsagents on the eastern side of Saturday Market near the Market Cross.

In the Town Trail booklet, we are told the design is taken from one of the misericords in Beverley Minster, but I think most of us would benefit from knowing a little more about its origins.

Misericords are hinged seats placed in the choir stalls of medieval churches. The name means 'mercy seat' because the user can put the seat down and prop his or her backside on it to obtain relief in the long periods of standing during the church service. Beverley Minster has sixty-eight choir stalls and sixty-eight mercy seats. Beneath each of them is a wooden carving. The carvings were placed there when the choir stalls were built in 1520. The subjects fall into several categories including heraldry, fools and follies, satires, bestiary (animals) and the world turned upside down (WTUD). However, the horse and cart is part of the 'proverbial follies' group and is said to be based on the proverb 'putting the cart before the horse' - meaning to do things in the wrong order or manner, or contrary to convention. The proverb was mentioned in Whittinton's Vulgaria (1520): 'That teycher setteth the cart before the horse that prefereth imitacyon before precepts', and twice in the English works of Sir Thomas More (c1530) under the striking heading 'arsy-versy': "Ye set the cart before the horse.....cleane, contrarily and arsy-versy".

Each of the misericords consists of three parts - a central carving with a supporter carving on each side - the 'Cartmen' installation is only the centre carving. The complete carving and its 'supporters' is shown

Beaver Carving from Beverley, Ontario, Canada

on page 124 and is equally intriguing. The right-hand supporter shows a maid milking a cow but when you look carefully the cow has no udder - so it is a bull and impossible to milk! I take it that the meaning is that of 'foolishness' or 'folly' just as with the 'cart before the horse'. The left-hand supporter has been described as 'cow lying down' or 'cow, recumbent, licking itself' - but, as the expert M.H.Jones says, it is clearly not a cow, but is identical to the bull in the right-hand supporter.

He is unable to explain any particular connotation! The misericords are intriguing - you must go and look at them. Before you do, read some of Malcolm Haydn Jones's thesis - heavy going but you can flick through the document in thirty minutes and get the ideas.

THE GLOVERS

Hand in glove and glove in hand,
Glovers were always in demand
Since The Middle Ages.

So many idioms used today
Refer to gloves in some way
In useful handy phrases.

When something fits just like a glove,
When rivals take their gloves off,
When things are treated with kid gloves,
The inference it rubs off.

And glove makers in our town,
Well served by local tanners,
Made gloves for those who did rough work
And those with gracious manners.

And on the Westwood were there jousts
And contests of high drama,
With gauntlets thrown by high-born maids
To knights in shining armour?

Art Installation number 7

THE GLOVE MAKERS

The word glove is Middle English and is derived from the Old English *glof*, or *glofa*, or the Old Norse *golf* - all meaning a covering for the hand. Personally, I rather like the German *handschuhe*, meaning shoe for the hand.

The term signifies a covering for the hand with separate sheaths for fingers and thumb - not to be confused with a fingerless glove (in USA, a 'mitt') or a 'mitten', which covers the entire hand with no sheaths and is warmer. Not to mention 3 finger gloves and the hybrids called 'glittens', where the finger covering can be detached or folded back!

Gloves were identified in Ice Age cave paintings, and a pair of linen ones were found alongside King Tutankhamun in his Egyptian tomb. In medieval times, before the C16th, they were mainly used in ecclesiastical situations (e.g. Mass), by royalty, at ceremonial events, by outdoor manual labourers and in falconry and archery.

The Glove Makers Guild received its first Royal Ordinance in 1347, and all gloves were handmade by its craftsmen and their apprentices until 1807, when an Englishman called James Winter of Stoke-Sub-Hamden invented a sewing machine for making gloves called a Glove Donkey. Working men's gloves were made of leather lined with cotton or knitted wool (a skill which required a five year Guild apprenticeship), whilst butlers, waiters and kitchen staff wore long white cotton gloves to protect their hands from heat.

A form of glove the 'gauntlet' - made of leather or metal armouring - was a feature of the fighting men throughout the Middle Ages. It was not until the end of the C15th that gloves took on the role of fashion accessories - and very expensive ones too, often with rich embroidery and jewelling. In the C18th soft leather 'chicken skin' gloves became popular - in fact they were made from the skin of unborn calves and were called 'limericks' after their place of origin. If that's not enough, then you might like to know that Shakespeare's father was a tanner and a glove maker, and 'glove silver' was a reward given to Officers of the Court.

Medieval Three Fingered Gloves -worn by the workers because they were simpler to make (therefore cheaper) and were said to be warmer because the fingers were next to each other.

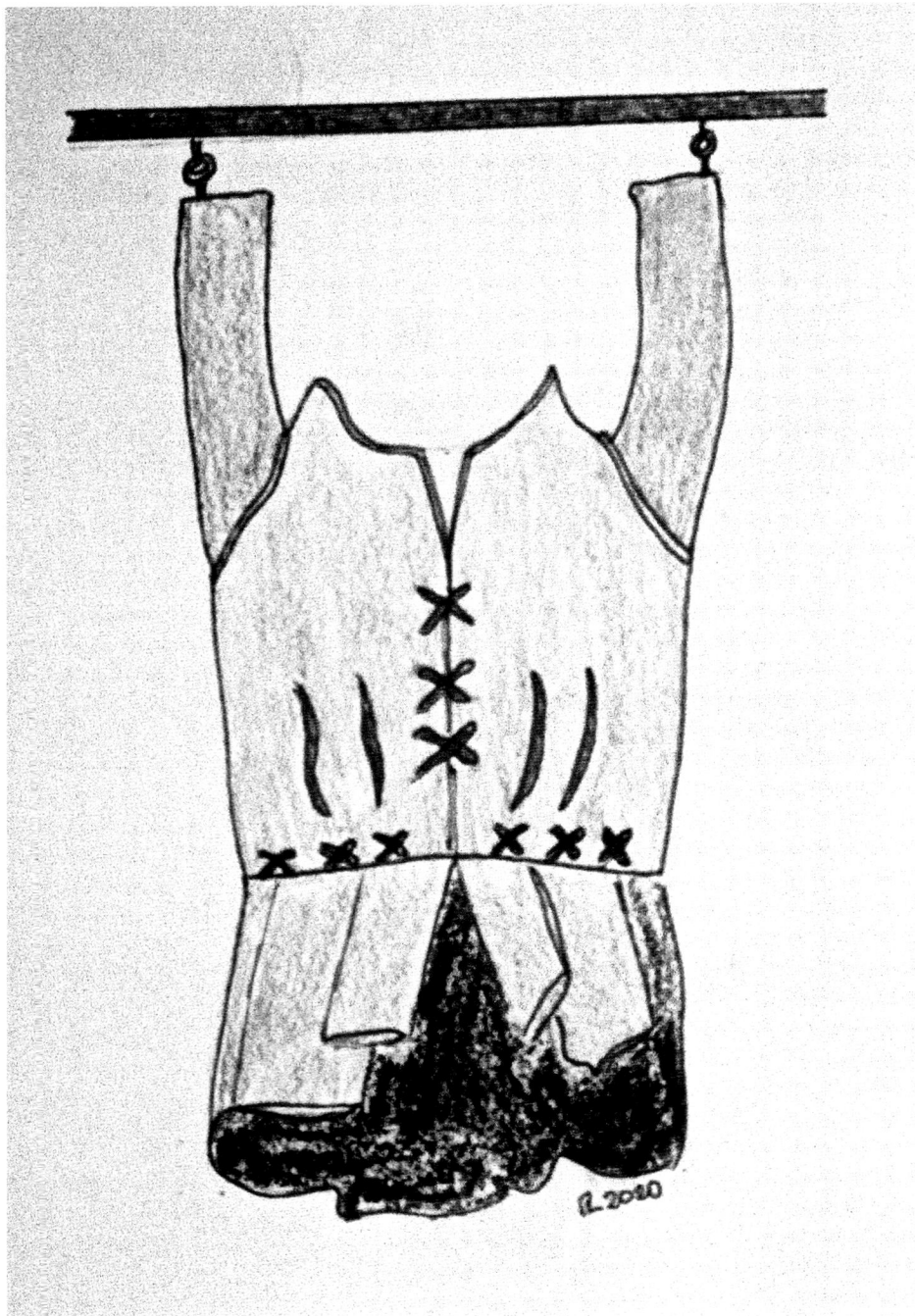

THE JERKIN MAKERS

The garment of the finest leather,
The fashionable jerkin,
With expert craftsmanship was made -
'Twas far too posh to work in.

And then there was the combat style,
Well-padded and full-sleeved,
An outer layer to take the blows
The foot soldier received.

The cordwainer, who made them both,
A man of devilish cunning,
Had products thus for war and peace
To keep his workshop running.

THE JERKIN MAKERS

Go and have a pint (or a gin if you prefer) in The Beaver on North Bar Within. The entrance is on the right side of the pub, just down Wheatsheaf Lane (formerly Suggitt's Lane). Look up - there is the jerkin suspended from the sky. Jerkins were worn throughout the Middle Ages by all segments of society including soldiers, peasants, bailiffs and huntsmen. They were like a vest or waistcoat, usually sleeveless and worn open or closed over a long-sleeved doublet or shirt. They were usually made of boiled leather which was more water resistant. Long sleeved jackets were used as armour; the short-sleeved ones were often decorated with holes and motifs made with a 'pinking iron'. Who made them? There was a group of leather workers who specifically made jerkins, but some were made by the cordwainers. By the late C16[th] and C17[th] jerkins became very ornate - often quite long and waisted, and sometimes made of wool and velvet - I suspect these were made by the tailors.

There is an article by Beatrice Behlen describing a C16[th] jerkin in the Museum of London. The title *A Jacket Well Examined* is taken from the works of French barber- surgeon Ambrose Pare, who disguised himself to hide during the siege of Hesdin in 1553 and wrote: "and for the fearr of being known I gave a velvet coate and Satin doublet to a Souldier who gave me a scurvy old torn doublet cut and slasht with using and **a leather jacket well examined** ……"

I think it fits in well with The Jerkin Makers.

A satin doublet by Sally Bell

The Minstrels in pastel by Helen Tojagic

THE MINSTRELS

In our Trail the crafts and trades, they number thirty nine,*
Like John Buchan's famous steps, an aide-memoire of mine.

Some trades have gone, the rest have changed - in fact it must be said
That only music still retains a long unbroken thread.

The choral music sung each day the Minstrels might have known,
Who perch on columns high above, their features carved in stone.

The Festivals held in our town, restored post Covid pause,
Successors to the Mystery Plays and their inheritors.

In our Trail the crafts and trades they form a proud tradition
In which the Minstrels and their lays still hold pole position.

* Time waits for no one, there are now 40 art installations

THE MINSTRELS

In the Minster there are seventy stone carvings of various medieval musical instruments including bagpipes, fiddles, tambourines, trumpets, flutes, pipes, a psaltery (stringed instrument of the zither family), cymbals and shawms (woodwind oboe-like instruments). A lot of these decorate the nave's north aisle but there are others in different places in the church - if you want to see them all, look at Gladys Strickland's article (referenced in sources). On the misericord seats there are five wood carvings showing musicians with instruments. In St Mary's there is the famous Minstrel's Pillar with its five musicians and their silver chains, as well as thirty-three other carvings with a musical theme.

All of this shows what an important part music played in medieval Beverley. But what I want to tell you about are the musicians/minstrels called the 'waites' (modern spelling 'waits'), who are recorded as being a feature of life in Beverley in the Middle Ages. At first it all seems straightforward: the waites originated as watchmen in camps, castles and other fortified places – blowing their horns as an alarm or signal of danger, or perhaps to mark the passing of the hours of the night (Walter Woodfall 1953). They then moved out into the cities and towns, accompanying the town watchmen and playing their instruments to warn of their coming. By the C15[th] they had metamorphosed into town employees as the town's musicians – playing pipes in the streets or at festive occasions. They wore special livery and silver chains (as depicted in the St Mary's Minstrel Pillar) and had their own Minstrels/Musicians Guild. OK, OK, so what's the fuss? Well, you need to look at Richard Rastall's treatise entitled '*The Origin of the Town Waits and the Myth of the Watchmen turned Musicians*'. He gets very hot under the collar (and probably quite rightly so) because people have perpetually mixed up the COURT or DOMESTIC wait employed in the nobility's castle, and the CIVIC or MUNICIPAL minstrel of the town, who he says never had a 'watchman' function. So, there you are!

Watch out for The Water Pump near The Minstrels,
beautifully restored courtesy of The Civic Society.

CHAIN MAIL LINO CUTTING   R 2021

THE ARMOURERS

The armourers or furbishers came from the metal trades,
The plumbers and the pewterers and the cutlers who made blades.

Steady lads in Civvy Street the metal bashing boys,
But once they heard the call to arms, the thunder and the noise,

'Twas to the chain mail benches, and grab the armour plate,
And " take his Lordship's measurements and of his horse's mate."

"Now thrive the armourers" said the Bard,
the Youth of England is a fire,
And we have weapons to repair for the yeoman and the noble squire.

Art Installation number 10

THE ARMOURERS

The type of armour or protection worn by the soldiers and knights of the Middle Ages was largely dictated by how much they could afford. The poorest soldiers might just wear a long **quilted jacket** which helped soften the blows but was little defence against high quality arrows and swords. The next step up was a jacket made of boiled leather - a process which made it very hard. This was called a '**cuir bouilli**' and could be worn over a quilted jacket or have strips of armour plate sewn on to it for added protection. **Chain mail** was in common use from the C3rd BC until C16th AD. A shirt of mail stretching to the knee was called a '**haubeck**' or, if it only covered to the thigh, a '**hauburgeon**' or '**byrnie**'. The mail was made of either a mixture of riveted and solid rings or just riveted rings alone (stronger). The rings were of either wrought iron or tempered steel of 14–18 gauge thickness in a 4:1 pattern i.e. each ring was linked to four others. The jacket might contain between fifteen and forty thousand rings and weigh up to 15kg (33 lbs).

Full body armour came into use in the late C14th and early C15th, and was used until the advent of gunpowder and explosive weaponry made it obsolete. A suit of armour could be new - either 'bespoke' or 'off the peg' - or second hand. A new suit cost upwards of £8 depending on its quality and decorations. This may not sound much but remember the average village thatcher craftsman made only about £8 a year. Made of tempered steel, the sheets were carefully jointed and articulated as freedom of movement was paramount. An average suit of armour weighed 15-25 kg (33-55 lbs). Getting into it required some practice and often help from the knight's squire. Under the armour the knight wore a quilted jacket with fastenings for some of the plates and a skirt of chain mail. The chest, abdominal and back plates were often in one piece and were slipped over the head. The arm, elbow, thigh, knee and lower leg protectors were strapped into place with leather straps.

I know what you are thinking - what did the poor knight do if he were desperate for the toilet? Well I suppose he could lift up the chain mail skirt, but might have to get his squire along to the remove the rear '**culet**'! A labelled suit of Gothic C16[th] armour is shown overpage. I have added a list of the various parts - just in case you did not know them! Finally, we must not forget the long, colourful surcoats worn over the armour and often depicting the knight's personal arms - so much a part of our schoolday image of the knights of the Wars of the Roses.

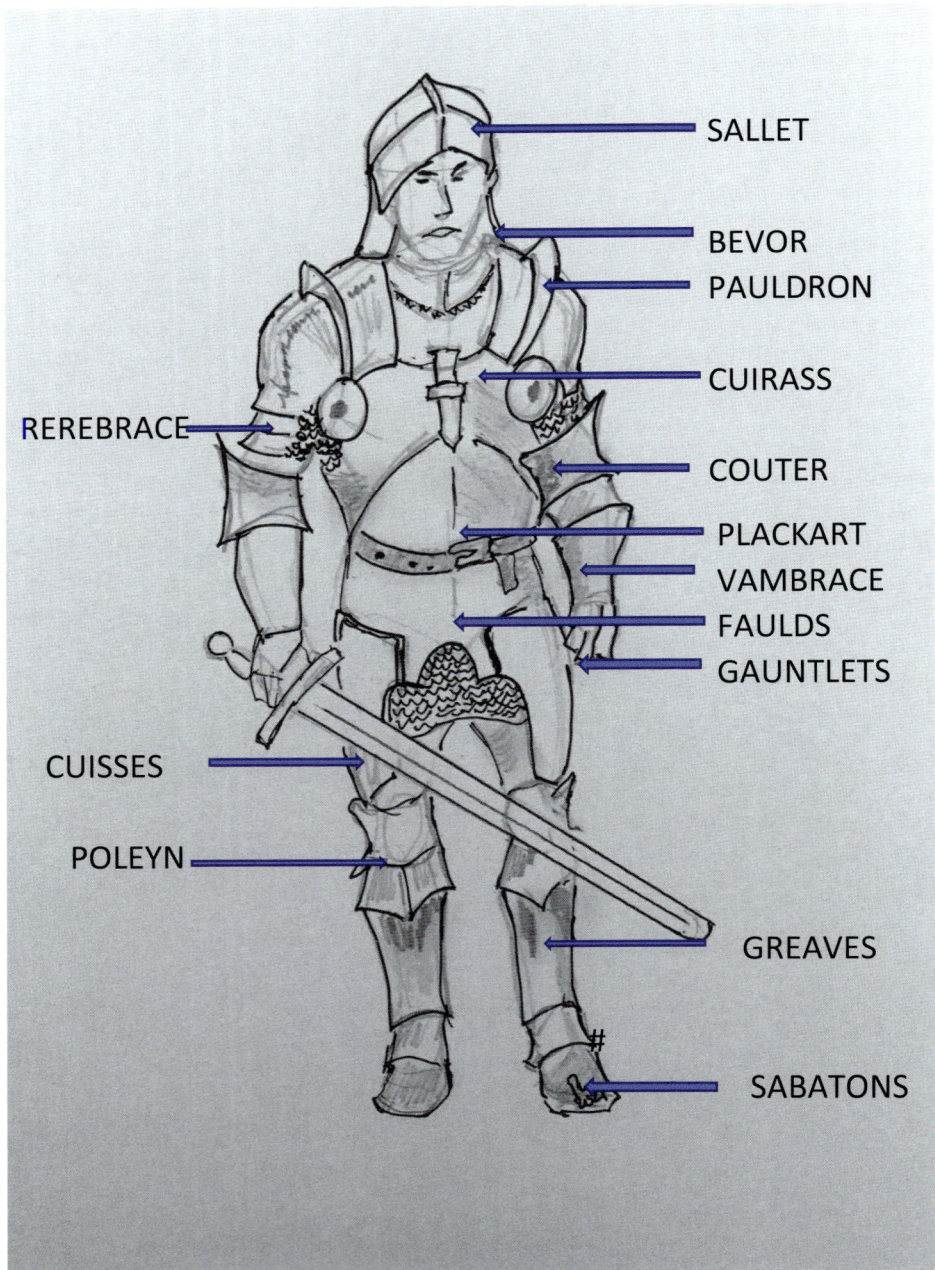

SALLET

BEVOR

PAULDRON

CUIRASS

REREBRACE

COUTER

PLACKART

VAMBRACE

FAULDS

GAUNTLETS

CUISSES

POLEYN

GREAVES

SABATONS

Sallet : Helmet

Bevor or **gorget**: steel or leather throat protection

Pauldron: covers the shoulder, armpit and back of neck

Spaulders: cover the shoulder - smaller than pauldron

Cuirass: breast plate - usually includes back plate as well

Rerebrace: protects the upper arms

Couter: curved metal plate protecting the elbow

Plackart: abdominal plate

Vambrace: forearm guard - made of boiled leather or steel

Faulds: plate armour below the breast plate protecting hips and waist

Gauntlets: protect hand and wrist

Cuisses: protect the thigh (French for thigh is cuisse)

Poleyn: protects the knee, also called **genouillere**

Greaves or **jambeaux:** protect the lower leg

Sabatons or **sollerets**: protect the foot

From North Bar Accounts 1409

To two bricklayers and their servants for one week
10 shillings

On Friday 9th August to bricklayers, their servants, six labourers one carter, and other small things reckoned together
32 shillings 10 pence

On the same day to Agnes the Tiler for 1,000 tiles
3 shillings 8 pence

Different tips given to the workmen and other small things
8½ pence

To another four bricklayers and one servant of them, deducting two days for which they were absent,
12 shillings

To the same bricklayers, and their servants for the week before the feast of All Saints reckoned together,
15 shillings

To William Potter for 4,000 tiles,
15 shillings 1 penny

THE BRICKLAYERS and THE TILERS

As we enter Westwood, upstairs on the bus,
There's a wonderful sight just waiting for us:

The Twin Towers of Beverley constructed in stone,
Stone from the West Riding, it wasn't our own.

But wait till the next stop, outside the Bar,
Those are our bricks, pal, yes they truly are.

The oldest brick entrance throughout the land
Sourced from local brickyards, we do understand.

Over one hundred thousand Beverley bricks
Laid by our own brickies, now them's statistics.

THE BRICKLAYERS and THE TILERS

The building trade commanded several different guilds including the Stonemasons, the Carpenters, the Pla(i)sterers, the Bricklayers, the Wallers, the Pavers and the Tilers. When any building was constructed, there was a defined 'pecking order' with the Master Builder at the top - he was usually a stonemason or carpenter and was responsible for the design and the build.

Anne Newsome tells us that before the C13th tilers were pretty low in the craftsmen's pecking order and were not allowed a guild; it was thought to be a dirty trade and the furnaces or kilns smelled badly. It is a little difficult to sort out, but it seems to me that before the C15th the tilers made roof tiles (called thakketyles) as well as bricks (called waltyles, or wall tiles).

After the C15th the bricklayers often broke away and had their own guild, although it is recorded that Kingston upon Hull had a well-established combined Guild of Tilers, Bricklayers and Wallers.

Just when you think you are getting it sorted out, remember that tilers in London were also called tylers, tyleres, tylans or tyghleres; in Lincoln they were called poyntons, in Cheltenham helliers and in some places slaters! Fortunately, it seems the 'brickies' were only called either bricklayers or wallers.

If you look closely at the reproduction of the North Bar account roll for 1409, shown previously, you will see that some of the tiles were bought from Agnes the Tiler. This is interesting because women were often not allowed to join guilds - usually only being a 'part member' if they had been widowed and were continuing to run their deceased husband's business. There were exceptions - where the craft was a 'domestic' activity such as spinning, silk making or brewing, then sometimes the butchers, ironmongers, shoemakers and goldsmiths would allow women members, but often with reduced privileges.

NORTH BAR

THIS BAR IS THE ONLY REMAINING ONE
OF THOSE WHICH FORMERLY GUARDED
THE MAIN ENTRANCES TO THE TOWN IT
WAS BUILT BY THE TOWN COUNCIL IN
1409 AT A COST OF £96-0-11.

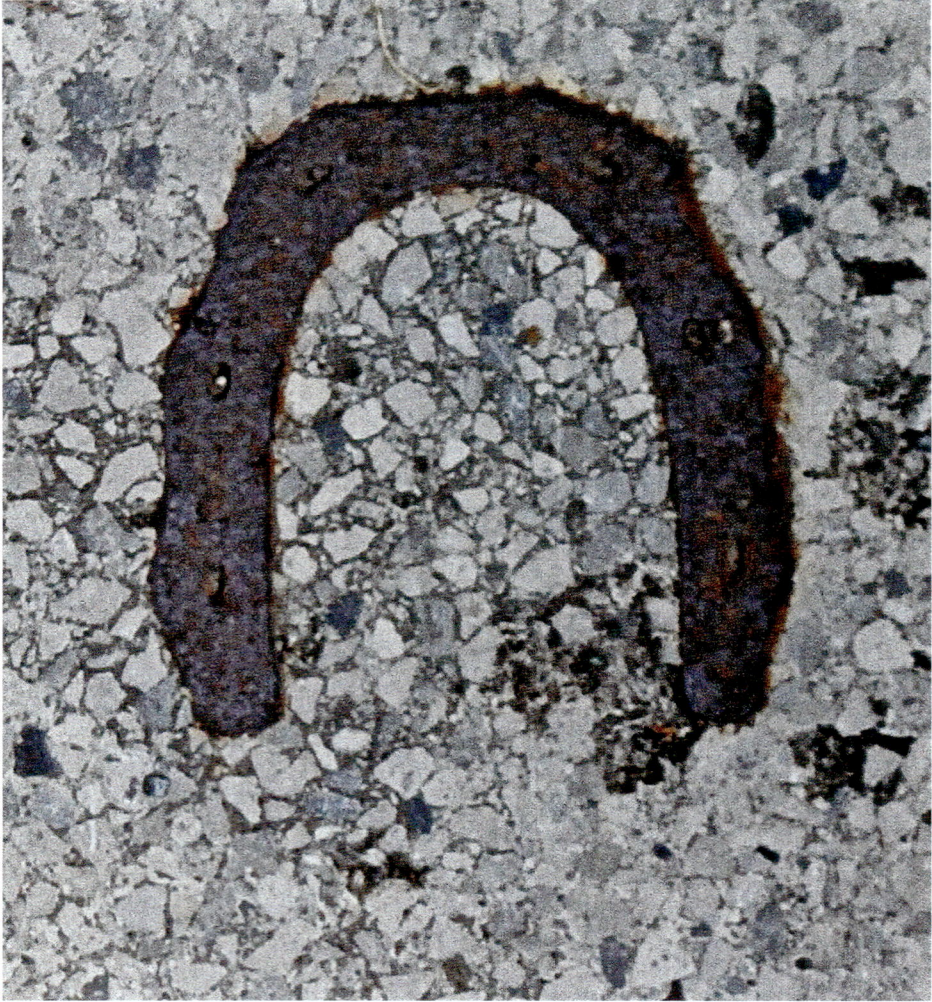

THE FARRIERS and THE LORIMERS
THE BOYS AND THE BLACKSMITHS

"There's horseshoes on the pavement -
Why aren't they on the flipping road?"
They said, to his amazement

Because there was no flipping road,
But just a muddy track
That led up to the Blacksmith's forge
And they were coming back

With brand new shoes upon their hooves
And trotting to their stables.
"We don't believe a word of that,
It's one of Grandad's fables".

From Sam and Ben visit Beverley - unpublished

Art Installation number 12

THE FARRIERS and THE LORIMERS

There is a bit of sorting out to do here. In medieval times what was the difference between a lorimer, a farrier and a blacksmith and how did they all fit into that wider group called 'the smiths'? Well, a **lorimer** was someone who made stirrups, spurs and other metal bits used with horses. A **farrier** (Latin root *ferrum* - or iron) made and fitted shoes for horses. A **blacksmith** was a smith who works with iron. The 'black' in his name refers to black fire scale or oxide, which forms on iron when it is heated. The 'smith' comes from the Old English word *smythe,* meaning to strike. A blacksmith may never have had contact with a horse, but lorimers and farriers needed training in blacksmithery.

They were all part of a large group of craftsmen called 'the smiths', who all worked with metal in some form or another, and would include locksmiths, goldsmiths, silversmiths (also called whitesmiths because they worked with 'white metals') and bladesmiths. In Beverley they were defined as 'any craftsmen working on an iron stethy'.

The blacksmith could be responsible for a large number of items, from household utensils and tools to farm machinery, weapons, armour and instruments of torture. He was regarded as part of the 'seven basic mechanical arts' and had to be skilled in the seven basic operations of forging - namely drawing down, shrinking, bending, upsetting, swaging, punching and forge welding.

In Beverley the lorimers worked on Lorimer Row, near where The Rose and Crown now stands on York Road. The type of bridles made were very similar to today's; the metal bits were made of iron, bronze or copper. The farriers (or marshals) worked on Farrier Lane in Eastgate.

Medieval horses were nearly always shod, the horseshoe nails being hand hammered and square. The holes in the horseshoe were also square and usually eight in number - so perhaps the horseshoes on York Road are not strictly correct!!

I am not sure where the blacksmiths' forges were, but Crafts and Trades in East Yorkshire tells of an old forge at Lund (now a bus shelter) and a blacksmith's shop at Swine. It also records this wonderful tribute to the blacksmith at Leven, inscribed on his gravestone:

"My anvil and my hammer lie neglected,

My bellows have lost their wind.

My fire's extinct, my forge decayed

And in the dust my vice is laid.

My coals are spent, my irons gone,

My last nail's drove, my work is done."

THE WINDMILLERS

The windmillers appeared just after the Normans
When the grinding of corn was quite a performance.

The first ones were fixed where the wind was expected
But it frequently failed to blow as directed.

Whence came the expression 'there's trouble at mill'
When the wooden sails stood regrettably still.

Now a thousand years later we're back where we started;
Those great cooling towers will soon be departed

And wind turbines stand where windmills once stood,
And the future is green and we hope that is good.

THE WINDMILLERS

The advantage of windmills over water mills was that they could function when the water supply was insufficient, so it is no surprise that windmills were erected on the slightly higher ground of Beverley Westwood.

Although the first mention of a windmill in Yorkshire was in 1185 at Weedley in South Cave, the first windmill on Westwood was probably not erected until 1646 and was called Hither Mill. Hither Mill was a 'post mill' - that is the whole body of the mill housing the machinery was mounted on a single vertical post so that the mill could be turned to bring the sails into the wind. The original wooden structure was replaced by a brick tower mill in 1773. Of the other windmills on Westwood, Black Mill was built by the council around 1654, Lowson's Mill in 1801, later followed by Fishwick's, Antimill (now the golf course club house) and a mill at the Whiting Works which ground chalk stone.

Some of the mills were built by private enterprise and fell into bankruptcy. When a mill became vacant or unusable the incoming tenant had to negotiate terms with the council. This provided a hidden benefit to the town as the rentals provided charity money to give the poor of the town a Christmas gift.

The story of Butt Close Mill is most interesting. On the condition that a mill was built on Butts Close - part of the old archery ground on the eastern boundary of Westwood - the Corporation issued a 99-year lease. In 1861 the then tenant, Mr Fishwick, with the Corporation's agreement, demolished the mill, stored the components, but retained his house and outbuildings. The freemen of Beverley (The Pasture Masters) were enraged and sent a number of their men around to regain the property - they sat around smoking their pipes and shouting ''we've cum to tak us rights''. Two police officers were unsuccessful in dispersing the mob, which then set fire to the property and mill remnants. Arrests were made and two of the ringleaders, Cherry and Duffil, were sent for trial at York and punished.

That must have taken 'the wind out of their sails'!

For the times they are a-changin': courtesy WikiCC

THE BAKERS

There's not too much that one can say
About the humble baker,
Except perhaps he has to be
A very early waker.

His maths don't have to be too good,
If you know what I mean -
Just ask him for a dozen buns,
I bet you get thirteen.

And yet he plays a crucial role,
For it must be said:
Where on earth would we all be
Without our daily bread?

THE BAKERS

Did you know that a round, flat and stale piece of bread was used as a plate to eat off in medieval times and was called a 'trencher'? Me, neither. As the food juices soaked through the bread it gradually became softer and thus more edible!

The baker was a very important person in the Middle Ages, but he was also a very highly regulated one. Each town would have a Bakers' Guild, and the products they produced were subjected to strict quality control by the wardens from the Merchants' Guild. The fines imposed for undercutting were so considerable that in an order of twelve loaves the baker would add in an extra one to be on the safe side. There you are then: 'a baker's dozen'. The bread made was usually unleavened - i.e. they did not use yeast. Finely ground, sifted wheat was used to make the white bread of the wealthy - called pandemain or manchet. The poorer people ate dark brown, hard bread made from rye or barley. Other ingredients were added to make it cheaper. 'Cheat' was wheat bread with bran, and 'horse bread' was any grain plus peas and beans and was not for the horses!

Finally, here is something which would not go down well in the woke society we now live in. The bakers made their loaf the size of one, normal adult portion. In polite society the gentlemen cut off the crusts and gave them to the women present, who dipped the crusts to make them easier to eat!

Tiger Lane

Stephen the Goldsmih

PL 2021

THE GOLDSMITHS

The Goldsmiths were, it is agreed, the very finest craftsmen
Because they really had to be metallurgists, artists, draughtsmen.

Each piece of work that they produced had a special hallmark,
The precious metals that they used must be in the right ballpark.

The leading Goldsmith of his day, a wealthy guy called Steve,
Was in the Minster Canon's pay, or so we all believe.

'Twas he who gave the Eastgate site to the Dominican Friars,
Ignoring the attractive bids of would-be High Street buyers.

But after seven hundred years his gift has been rewarded,
Thanks to the Trail Committee's team who've had the facts recorded.

And on a pavement within the Bar, you'll find inscribed his name,
Glorified for evermore … at the bottom of Wood Lane.

THE GOLDSMITHS

So what is it that makes gold so special to the world of art and jewellery? Firstly, it is in short supply, so it is valuable. It does not corrode or tarnish, it is easy to melt and forge, it is malleable and ductile and, above all else, it looks beautiful. A little can go a long way - an ounce of gold (28 grams) can be beaten into a thin sheet measuring three hundred square feet.

The medieval times were good ones for the goldsmith. The demand for beautiful objects for the churches, requests for intricate jewellery by royalty and the rich, and the market for engraved manuscripts made his craft a busy and a lucrative one. In his apprenticeship the trainee goldsmith was taught sawing, cutting, forging, melting, soldering. enamelling and engraving. Frequently these skills were handed down from father to son, while the ladies of the family did the polishing and ran the shop.

The variety of techniques used by the medieval craftsmen are fascinating and included 'chasing' - in which a sunken design was hammered out of a metal sheet - and the popular reverse of this, a 'repousse' - when the back of the sheet is hammered to produce an elevated low relief design. Intricate enamelling was used for jewellery and church artefacts, as was the technique of filagree, or granulation, in which complex designs were made by chains of tiny gold beads or gold globules. Perhaps the most intriguing technique of all was 'chryselephantine' art (from the Greek *chrysos* for gold and *elephantinos* for ivory), in which gold and ivory were blended to create intricate designs or sculptures.

Records show that the Minster employed its own goldsmiths - Stephen the Goldsmith around 1240, and Richard the Goldsmith, who was the brother of William de la Mere, the Minster Provost, around 1338. But the new shrine for Saint John's relics (1296) was an 'out of house' contract fulfilled by Richard of Farringdon, a London goldsmith.

The Goldsmiths' Guild in Beverley was an important one, and their contribution to the Guild plays was, appropriately, 'The Three Wise Men'.

Saint Eligius, Patron Saint of Goldsmiths (en.numista.com)

THE HATTERS

As a rule of thumb, it used to be said,
The finer the hat, the nobler the head.

Whereas the flat cap, the choice of the poor,
Was simpler to make and cheaper for sure.

But a problem arose upon All Fools' Day,
When a cap trimmed with bells was much on display.

Which led to a crisis in millinery matters,
When the cappers fell out with their colleagues the hatters.

The cappers accused of lowering the tone,
Decided to form a branch of their own.

You stick to your posh hats, we'll stick to our bells,
For when all's said and done it's the Jester's cap sells.

MEDIEVAL HATS

SUMMER STRAW PEASANT HAT

WINTER FELT HAT

WIMPLE HEADDRESS
C2 - C4

LADIES BUTTERFLY HAT

LADIES STEEPLE HAT

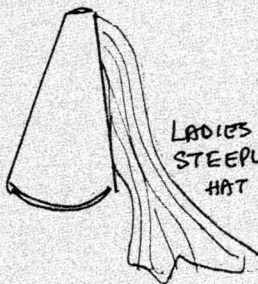
HOODY!

PLUMED FELT HAT

C4 COIF

R 2021

168

THE HATTERS

You would think it was a simple matter making hats in medieval times. Not so. There were **haberdashers** who made and sold all the accessories for clothes but also dabbled in hats, and the **feltmakers** who provided the hat material. Then amongst these Guilds there were the **cappers** or **cappemakers,** the **hatters** (derived from Latin *capellarius* and French *chapelier*) and also the **hurers,** who made the thickening or fulling materials. There was good money in hats as everyone wore them, so it is not surprising there were squabbles amongst the craftsmen. Why were hats so popular?

Well, they had religious connotations, they kept the hair more hygienic, protected from the sun in summer and the wind and rain in the winter and, very importantly, reduced the spread of lice! Only later in the Middle Ages did they become symbols of fashion and wealth amongst the nobility.

What did they wear?

In the early Middle Ages 'coifs' made of linen were worn by men and women, rich and poor. These were helmets of linen worn tight to the hair and tied under the chin with a string or straps. Poor people used unbleached, undyed linen; the wealthy bleached, fine linen. The ladies also wore 'wimples' made of linen or silk, which covered the neck and chin and often the head - much in the way of today's hijab. In the summer, men would wear straw brimmed hats or hoods with a long tail and felt, wide brimmed hats in the winter. In the later Middle Ages ladies' hats became a symbol of high fashion and wealth, as the wearers sought to outdo each other. The butterfly hats with their starched linen wings and the 'steepled' hats will be examples we remember from medieval portraits. Finally a word about the jester and his hat. The jester was employed by a nobleman or monarch to provide amusement and fun for him and his guests and was part of the household - I suppose our modern-day equivalent would be the circus clown. Jesters were also itinerants, appearing at markets and fairs. The jester wore a tight-fitting suit with different coloured legs and arms. The well-known jester's hat was also called a cockscomb or cap 'n' bells. It had three points (liliripes) representing the ears of an ass. The bells on his hat and costume were there to announce his presence, or that he was ready to 'mate'!!! Sometimes an ass's tail was added to his costume. He carried a mock sceptre known as a bauble in one hand, on the top of which was either a carved wooden head or an inflated animal bladder. So, there we are indeed, I jester not.

ALMOST THERE

Well done, you've almost walked 'all four'-
I bet your feet are pretty sore.
We hope you think it's been worthwhile,
Had some fun, had a smile,
Enjoyed it all and maybe
Caught a glimpse of historee.
So spread the word and tell the tale,
For you are now all Friends of the Trail.

So speaketh the Poet of Pasture Terrace,
So many words, so much to tell us.
The poems of this book, are all his work*-
Amusing, educational, some with a quirk.
I think they make this book unique:
Forty plus poems, what a feat.
Thank you Peter for what you've written,
A gift you have, so freely given.

(*excepting the prologue written by Tom Lee
and the epilogue by Berna Moody)

172

THE BOWYERS and the FLETCHERS

The Plantagenet Kings were a troublesome lot
Causing havoc both sides of the Channel;
Spending the money they clearly ain't got,
Experts in fake news and flannel.

They needed an army they couldn't afford -
Well equipped, reliable and steady,
To follow the Standard at home and abroad,
Self trained, self-funded and ready.

At the heart of it all was the English Longbow,
A fearsome and deadly weapon,
As the Archers let all their arrows go
To fall like a bolt from heaven.

The Archery Field was their practice ground
Where the skills of their trade were taught;
Such were the places the heroes were found
For Crecy and Agincourt.

THE BOWYERS

The Middle Ages were times of much conflict including the battles with the Scots and the War of the Roses, so the skills of the bowyers in providing the bows were much in demand. The Bowyers featured regularly in the town's annals and together with the Fletchers had their own Guild.

The preferred wood for the bows was yew, cut into a D shaped profile and varying in length from five to six feet. The 'nocks' at the top and bottom of the bow to which the strings were attached were made of horn and the strings themselves of linen flax, grown locally in Beverley. The cost of a bow was about twelve pence and was paid for by the town if the archer did not have his own bow. All adult males from the age of twelve years onwards were required to practise their archery skills every Sunday morning and on feast days as well.

The training areas were called the Butts - there were two of these in Grovehill which survived until the 18[th]C, one on the Westwood and almost certainly one on Butt Lane. The name originally referred to the mounds of earth at the end of the shooting field which were used as targets, and should not be confused with the American slang for your bum!

On going to war each mounted man was accompanied by two archers (yeomen) who were provided with a uniform that consisted of a jacket of either undyed wool or blue dyed wool or a mixture of both. On the jacket, as a means of identification, they wore a 'cognisance' or badge coloured red, yellow and green - all of which helped to prevent friendly fire. Most archers wore a metal hat, or a cap of boiled hide sometimes covered with pitch. Spare bowstrings were stored under the hat to keep them dry. When the Kings of England issued a call to arms, the town was expected to provide a levy of between 20 and 120 yeomen and they would be sent off with great civic pride from the Guildhall with a review on Westwood. Raising this number followed a well-ordered path! Firstly, any fit prisoners were released from jail to go and fight together with as many poachers as they could get - men who would already have acquired shooting skills. Next would come those men of the town known to be skilled archers - incidentally, a general pardon was issued to any archer practising on the Butts who killed anyone!

With the increased use of protective armour and later of explosives, the use of archers slowly declined but it remained a popular sport. Just to cheer you up, it is said that when the Queen of England (Anne Boleyn) was executed for treason in 1536 her body was put into an elm box made for arrow sheaths.

*Art Installation number 17*_

THE FLETCHERS

Every bow needs an arrow. The fletchers made these, whether they were for long bows, short bows, cross bows and for hunting or battle.

Trade was good for the fletchers in the Middle Ages. In 1359, during the 100 Years War with France, 850,000 arrows were delivered to the Royal Armoury in the Tower of London. The materials needed for arrows were also stored in the Tower - indeed in 1417 it was declared that six feathers from every goose killed had to be sent to the Armouries, with the counties being told they had to provide 1,190,000 goose feathers the next year!

So we need to know a bit about medieval arrows. At one end is the arrowhead, made of forged metal (iron or later steel). In the early Middle Ages, the arrows were called broadheads. They were flat and had barbs on both sides to do more damage on entry and removal. These arrows were used for both hunting and battle as they would pass through cloth and flesh but were no use against armour. Later, longer and narrower arrowheads were introduced which could pierce armour and chain mail (called bodkins).

Next up comes the shaft which was made of different types of wood, but preferably poplar or ash, and rounded in shape. At the other end was the 'fletching' or stabiliser, made of goose feathers and fixed to the arrow by skin glue with a whipping of silk or linen thread. A notch or 'nock' was made in the end of the arrow to engage the bowstring. This was very important in correctly rotating the arrow and preventing it slipping during drawback and release. The classic treatise on medieval arrows is called 'Toxophilus' (The Schole of Fhootinghe Contayned in Tvvo Bookes) published by Roger Ascham in 1545.

In Beverley the Fletchers were closely allied to the Bowyers and joined with them in performing the play 'Abraham and Isaac' on Corpus Christi Day. The play was performed on a wooden castle erected at the bullring and placed opposite the castle of the Butchers' Guild. The event took place over two days beginning on Rogation Sunday.

Medieval Longbowmen Wiki commons

BEVERLEY TOWN TRAIL: THE EPILOGUE

When through these streets that twist and twine
That link the churches tall and fine
Our feet lead us where men of old
Carried their burdens to make their gold.
Craftsmen in workshops toiled and wrought
With stone and metal, wood so sleek,
They held their markets every week
Where food and drink and goods were bought.
If feeling hungry pies were sold
And ale to wash down dusty throats,
A hat, a glove, a shoe or gown,
A fish, a dish, a lock, a key,
A candle bright to light the night
A herb to cure a wounded knee.
Your horse has stumbled, here's a chap
To shoe anew and put you back.
We'll make some armour strong and bright
Some bows and arrows, set you right,
The King needs men, the Scots are coming,
We'll set off soon, the whole town's humming.
The women stay indoors and spin
They keep us clothed, neat as a pin,
They dye cloth bright in red and blue
With madder, woad and alum too.
When all is done and hands at rest
We'll settle down we've done our best.

We act our parts in mystery plays and pass our time in
pleasant ways,
We live our lives here in the town,
At dusk we turn to home and friends.
Our bones lie snug under the ground
Our names forgotten, deeds as well,
But you live on our tale to tell.
Remember us as you pass by -
Our songs, our lives, our loves don't die.

Berna

ACKNOWLEDGEMENTS

Thank you to the Town Trail Committee for their permission to base this book on the Trail and to our co-authors for allowing us to make free use of their original guide. Thank you to ERYCC for their support and, in particular, to Sharron Wilson who acted as the liaison. Thank you especially to our friends and family (shown above) who have contributed their time, paintings, poems and photographic skills (Nel King and Bob Aveyard) and made this book special to us. Chris Herman has spent hours proof reading and punctuating the text, and without the skills and experience of Richard Clough, Steve Waddington and the team at Hart and Clough this book would never have come to fruition. Lastly thank you to all the authors and sources of information we have listed. If we have missed anyone out or there are errors we apologise - please let us know.

INVITED CONTRIBUTIONS:

Thank you:

Sally Bell of Beverley for The Spinners and Medieval Jacket

Dr. Stephen Hill of Beverley for The Water Millers

Mary Laycock of Vancouver Island, BC, for The Wildfowlers

Helen Tojagic of Beverley for The Minstrels and The Creeler

Benjamin Lee of Newcastle for The Jester and The Fish

Samuel Lee of Newcastle for The Breadcake

Dr. Tom Lee of Newcastle for The Prologue

Katy Marriott of Beverley for The Beaver

Berna Moody of Beverley for The Epilogue

Cherry Polglase of Melbourne, Australia for The Barber Surgeon

Pam Wilkinson of Beverley for The Brewers

Pamela Hopkins wrote the scripts for The Rope Makers and The
Masons. Berna Moody wrote the scripts for The Windmillers and the
Fletchers and The Bowyers.

Pamela and Berna wrote The Water Millers.

Sadly, Ray Grange, who was Chairman of The Trail Committee, has
recently died. He did so much for The Trail's inception and continuation
and was very helpful in the planning of this book. I am sorry that he
didn't see its completion, I think he would have liked it. [PL Feb 2022]

HELP!
I CANNOT FIND THE ART INSTALLATION

WALK 1:

No 6 The Cartmen: Stand in Saturday Market opposite the Market Cross on the right hand side towards St Mary's Church. Face the front of Market News shop. Look down and The Cartmen installation is on a paving stone next to a big grate (measures only 12"X9" - not easy to see).

No 7 The Glovers: Walk up the right hand side of Saturday Market from Cartmen towards St Mary's. At top of market, look for the bench in front of Beercock's Estate Agency/Prescott's Jewellers. The glove is on the right hand arm of the bench as you face it.

No 8 The Jerkin Makers: Walk out of Saturday Market into North Bar Within on the righthand pavement towards North Bar. In 35 yards is The Beaver Pub on the right side of which is Wheatsheath Lane. Stand in the entrance to the Lane and look up, The Jerkin is suspended high up from a gantry.

No 9 The Minstrels: Walk about 120 yards from The Beaver towards the Bar crossing Hengate. Pass the church gate, then at the St Mary's Church notice board stop facing the wall and look down and left, the three Minstrels are on the paving stones.

No 10 The Armourers: Cross the road onto the left hand side of North Bar Within. Walk towards The Bar and immediately after you have crossed Tiger Lane (2 yards), look down at the pavement in front of the first shop window of St Mary's Court Shopping Arcade. The small square of chain mail is set in the pavement. Beware - looks a lot like a manhole or drain cover!!

No 11 The Tilers and Bricklayers: Walk about 100 yards towards the Bar. Stop in front of the door of The Bar House immediately before the grey arch. Look down and the Account Roll for 1409 is set in the pavement immediately adjacent to the wall of the right arch of the Bar (which bears a green historical plaque).

No 12 The Farriers and the Lorimers: Walk under the archway and turn left into York Road (opposite the Rose and Crown pub). Keep on the left pavement. About 25 yards up is the first of a series of horseshoes set into the pavement.

No 13 The Windmillers: Walk 100 yards up York Road and turn left into Pasture Terrace (opposite the Pasture Masters Lodge) - 25 yards up on left hand side is the Windmill art form.

No 14 The Bakers: Walk up Pasture Terrace (bearing right) for 100 yards. Turn left into Tiger Lane. Passing Tiger Lane Stables on your left, walk about 160 yards past a courtyard. On the road, behind a brick buttress and next to the double yellow lines, is the Baker's breadcake or loaf.

No 15 The Goldsmiths: Walk 55 yards to the junction of Tiger Lane with North Bar Within and turn right into North Bar Within, retracing your steps but on opposite side to The Minstrels. Pass in front of the Beverley Arms Hotel, cross entrance to Wood Lane and then almost immediately look down at pavement in front of the first shop (currently Nanini's). At the foot of the pillars (currently grey and yellow) is the art installation plate Stephen the Goldsmith.

No 16 The Hatters: Walk 50 yards further and cross Lairgate at the traffic lights to the 'tongue' of pavement leading into Saturday Market. Look for the signpost pointing to Lairgate shops. Sat on the top of it is the multicoloured Jester's cap.

No 17 The Bowyers and the Fletchers: Walk down the right hand side of Saturday Market until you come to Old Waste which joins Saturday Market to Lairgate. Cross Old Waste and stand in front of the shop looking at the red brick building of the HSBC Bank. There you will see the silver arrows of the art form.

WALK 2:

No 21 The Merchants: Stand on pavement on Champney Road opposite the Treasure House/Library. Walk 50 yards to the roundabout in front of the Magistrates Court. Turn left into Cross Street. 25 yards up on left in a small square is the Merchants.

No 22 The Fish Traders: Go back down Cross Street for 25 yards to roundabout in front of Magistrates Court. Turn left into Well Lane. Walk up left hand pavement for 85 yards. At the pedestrian zone sign look down and you will see the first eel. Walk 50 yards further towards Butcher Row and you will see five more eels.

No 1 The Butchers: Turn left in front of M and S and walk 50 yards up Butchers Row until you see The Angel pub. Turn into Angel Square. Twenty yards in front of you in the middle of the Square you will see the brown sculpture of the Ox.

No 2 The Walkers: Return to Butcher Row and walk right for forty eight yards until you see the sign Walkergate. Turn into Walkergate, the first footstep is on the pavement in front of the side window of Hugh Rice Jewellers. Walk up left side of Walkergate and you will see twelve more footprints. Walk 300 yards until you see the sign Swabys Yard.

No 3 The Cordwainers: is on the ground on your right on a little cobblestone area to the right of Walkergate House. If you can see Tesco's you've gone too far!

No 4 The Spinners: Retrace your steps and go up Swabys Yard. In 30 yards you will see the stainless steel spiral of the Spinners in front of Beverley Camera Shop. Walk left out of the yard past the micropub and under the arch until you meet Dyer Lane.

No 5 The Dyers: Turn right into Dyer Lane towards Saturday Market and in 38 yards you will see the Madder on a paving stone just before junction with the Market. Keep left and cross Saturday Market towards Toll Gavel. Stop at the signpost (fingerpost) at the entrance to Toll Gavel.

No 18 The Tailors: Look on top of the signpost (fingerpost) and you will find the first thimble. Walk across Toll Gavel to the first bench and you will find the second thimble on the pavement behind the right rear stanchion (very small – 2 cms. and dirty). On top of the left hand arm of the second bench you will find the third thimble.Look up Toll Gavel and 3 yards in front of the second bench on the pavement is the fourth thimble. Cross to the window in front of the shop which was once Burtons Tailors (7 yards in front of the second bench and 1 yard back) and the fifth thimble is on the pavement. Walk 10 yards up Toll Gavel and in front of the door into Carluccio's is the sixth thimble. Well done!

No 19 The Apothecaries: Walk 90 yards up the left hand side of Toll Gavel until you come to the gates of Toll Gavel United Church. On the left on a paving stone in front of the church notice board is the **Fevertree** design. Walk 25 yards further up and on the pavement in front of the menswear shop is **Eyebright.** Cross to other side of Toll Gavel and walk back to Landress Lane. On the pavement to right of Landress Lane is the **Cinquefoil** design - note it is about 1 yard from shop front nearer the central paving. Walk back up 13 yards and on right under the Hotel Chocolat window is **Coltsfoot**. At the present time due to wear and tear none of these are easy to find!!!

No 20 The Barber Surgeons: Walk 89 yards further up Toll Gavel keeping on the right side. On what is now the EE phone shop you will see two black and white snakes on the door posts. Walk further up Toll Gavel until you see the lamp post between the two benches at the junction of Toll Gavel with Cross Street. Look carefully at the top of the lamp post and you will see the curled snake.

WALK 3:

If you are proceeding to **WALK 3** then walk up Toll Gavel into Butcher Row and on into Wednesday Market.

No 23 The Printers: Highgate commences at the top right corner of Wednesday Market facing the Minster. Walk down the right hand pavement of Highgate for 150 yards passing the Monks Walk pub on your left. On the pavement in front of the Minster Vicar's house are the two squares of The Printers.

No 24 The Masons: Walk 70 yards down to the end of Highgate and turn left in front of the Minster to enter Minster Yard North. 20 yards down on the left in a little garden is the stone block of the art form. Walk 90 yards down Minster Yard North to Eastgate. Turn right into Eastgate and walk in front of the East Face of the Minster, in 50 yards veer right into Minster Yard South. In 130 yards (in front of the South face of the Church) before you come to St John Street, cross the road onto the grass verge in front of a field.

No 25 The Brewers: The six engraved flagstones of the Brewers can be seen on the verge in front of the Civic Society Information sign. The stones are numbered 1-6 with no.1 nearest St John Street.

No 26 The Carpenters: Turn round and walk back past the Brewers stones keeping on the right pavement. When Minster Yard South meets Flemingate the Carpenter's wood joint is in the pavement in front of you (immediately opposite across the road is The Sun Inn). Cross Flemingate and walk left back into Eastgate.

No 36 The Scriveners: 45 yards up Eastgate on the left is the entrance to Friary Lane. Cross this and in 20 yards you are in front of the Scriveners gate.

No 37 The Locksmiths: Walk up Eastgate towards Wednesday Market keeping on the right pavement. Go for 50 yards and you will come to an archway. Turn right under the archway and walk across the square until you see a blue sign "The Cloisters". Turn left down the little passageway into Paradise Square. Walk past the intriguing sculpture " The Jesters" by Jacqueline Gruber- Stieger and on your left is the Locksmiths artform on the adjacent low walls - ''Love laughs at Locksmiths''.

No 38 The Chandlers (candlemakers): Exit Paradise Square at top right into Outer Trinities. Walk 100 yards and in front of you is a decorative clock with a beaver on its weathervane. Set around it on the ground are the 'hour candles'. Walk across the ''square'' and turn left into Railway Street - signposted Treasure House /Town Centre - Walk down left side of Railway Street past New Walkergate on the right until you reach Wednesday Market.

No 39 Fishmonger: Cross the zebra crossing into the Market and on a paving in front of you is the Perch, in 3 yards the Herring, in 5 yards the Roach and finally in front of H. Peck and Sons is the Brill.

Walk 4 :

Start at Flemingate on the opposite side of the road to The Sun Inn (just around the corner from the Carpenters exhibit of Walk 3). Walk up the right-hand side and cross the railway line. In 150 yards pass the big Jewson sign. In 40 yards just before the entrance to the Leisure Centre/Potting Shed pub look up and you will see the saddle of **No 27 The Sadler** silhouetted against the sky. Walk up another 150 yards staying on the right hand side of Flemingate and on the pavement in front of No 62 (opposite the zebra crossing) is **No 28 The Weaver** art form – small, only 12" by 12". Walk on a further 145 yards and on the pavement in front of RM Motorcycle Repairs is **No 29 The Ropemakers** design (6 'long). Staying on the right side walk 150 yards until you have just passed The Sloop pub. Cross the road to the foot of the Beck and in front of The Foresters Arms you will see the statue of **No 30 The Creeler.** (If you have time, go up the right side of the waterway and look at the beautifully restored barge the MV Syntan - open at weekends in the summer). From the Creeler statue, cross Blucher Lane, walk 16 yards forward and the greylag goose of **The Wildfowlers** is in the garden on your right just beside the road sign for Blucher Lane. Walk back towards the Minster, but now on the right side of first Beckside and then Flemingate. In 120 yards you will come to Potter Hill. Cross the road in front of the beautiful clock on Legacy Funeral Directors and you will find **No 32 The Potters** installation on the pavement four yards in front of the corrugated fence on your right. Walk back down Flemingate about 150 yards and on the pavement in front of house number 63 you will see **No 32 The Water Millers**. Walk back towards the Minster staying on the right-hand side. When you come to the big roundabout at the entrance to the Flemingate shopping centre (opposite the Potting Shed) cross the road and on the wall immediately in front of you is **No 40 The Cooks** installation. Walk to your right - away from Flemingate in front of the Premier Inn, and in 60 yards cross the zebra crossing and walk down the gap into the Flemingate shops. Turn left and walk forwards 110 yards to Starbucks. Under the signpost pointing to bus station /railway station is **No 34 The Tanners** art form. Walk straight up, with Starbucks on your right, until you come to Armstrong Way (50 yards). Turn left and walk 60 yards to junction with Flemingate. Cross the road and, keeping to the right-hand side, cross the railway lines and in about 100 yards on the pavement in front of the Lord Nelson pub is **No 35 The Coopers** installation.

APPENDIX 1

APOTHECARY : Herbs and plants in medieval times and today

LAVENDER: used as an oil or flower grind in medieval times for headaches, migraine and epilepsy and as an antiseptic. Today is thought to have anticonvulsant, anxiolytic and sedative effects and is used in aromatherapy.

The white OPIUM pod was used as a mixture called DWALE along with other ingredients such as hemlock, henblane, animal bile, vinegar and wild lettuce as an anaesthetic before surgery e.g. limb amputation. Today opium is the source of morphine and heroin.

PEPPERMINT : often drunk as a tea in the Middle Ages for stomach complaints and indigestion. Today it is used in the treatment of heartburn and irritable bowel syndrome.

MARIGOLD : *Calendula* or Pot marigold was used for improving eyesight and withdrawing evil humours from the head. As late as the 1st World War it was still being used for its antiseptic properties. In Mexico the flowers are placed on graves on the Dia del Meurtos (Day of the Dead) as they are thought to lure souls back from the dead.

FOXGLOVE: used externally in the olden days for the treatment of ulcers and wounds. It was first mentioned in 1526 by one Peter Traveris for the treatment of 'feebleness of the heart'. Today it is the source of digitoxin and widely used in the treatment of heart failure and atrial fibrillation.

APPENDIX 2

MEDIEVAL GRAFFITI

Today the word graffiti conjures up the often lurid, multicolour writings seen on motorway bridges and the walls and sidings alongside our railway lines, or maybe even the spectacular drawings of the 'street artist' Banksy.

It is perhaps comforting to find that graffiti was rampant in medieval times. Like me, you probably wondered about the 'hieroglyphics' inscribed on the stone in the little garden set back on Minster Yard North. These are "masons marks" from the Minster and are part of the spectrum of medieval graffiti. The stonemasons were paid 'by piece' - the more they carved the more they were paid, so the marks meant they received their true recompense. In addition they served as quality control - if the carving was not up to scratch (pun intended) the master mason would know who was responsible.

The world of medieval graffiti is, however, much more complex and fascinating. Included are the multitude of religious protection symbols and carvings which have come to light on the walls of so many of our beautiful old churches and on the beams and fireplaces of ancient medieval buildings. Religious protection marks, also called "witches' marks" or apotropaic marks (from the Greek *apotropaios* meaning 'to turn away evil'), were part of medieval superstition and magic and were carved to add spiritual protection and ward off evil from the church or building. Apotropaic markings typically take one of three forms - a compass drawn design (hexafoil or daisy wheel), a pentacle (five pointed star) or a 'VV' symbol.

The Daisy Wheel, Hexfoil or Hexafoil
This common medieval graffiti protection mark takes the form of a six lobbed flower pattern drawn either singly or with multiple interlocking geometric shapes. Found in large numbers on the stonework of medieval built churches, it has been suggested that the mark is derived from the church consecration cross. Others would have it that the marks are purely the work of the stonemasons building the church, who would have access to a compass and could have used the design to train their

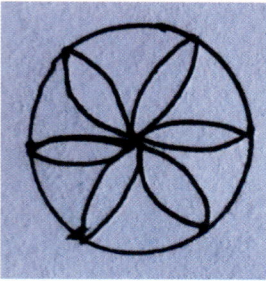

apprentices. The sheer volume of such marks, found not only in churches but also in houses and on furniture, would seem to mitigate against this and suggests they were made not by just masons and builders but by common folk perhaps using readily available household shears. Why should the hexfoil design be used to ward off evil spirits? In Pagan religions the hexfoil represents the sun - a source of good luck. In Christianity it is related to the Holy Trinity of the Christian faith with the support and help the Trinity brings with it. Or perhaps it is just because the daisy wheel is an example of an 'endless line' which the evil spirit is enticed to follow but from which it will never emerge?

The Pentangle

Mathew Champion tells us that the five pointed star or pentangle is found less commonly but is important because more is known about its significance and the reasons for its choice as a protection mark. In Grecian history it was a symbol of mathematical perfection, while post Reformation the star became associated with magic and in particular with the dark art of 'black magic' or Satanism. In medieval times, however, it was a Christian symbol. Much of the star's relevance might come from the poem 'Sir Gawain and the Green Knight' in which, as I am sure you will remember, the knight's shield bears the pentangle symbol engraved in pure gold on its face. The 5 pointed star brings protection to the knight in 5 ways: the 5 wounds Christ suffered on the cross, his 5 faultless fingers, the 5 senses, the 5 joys of the Virgin Mary in her Son and lastly the five 5 virtues of knighthood. The poet also tells us that the pentangle was regarded as the symbol of Solomon, and amongst other powers gave Solomon power over demons and protection from them. All of this was powerful ammunition for the medieval man or woman to use the symbol as a means of protection from evil.

The VV Symbol

The VV symbol is traditionally associated with the Virgin Mary and stands for Virgo Virginum (Virgin of Virgins). It sometimes appears as an M (Mary or Maria) or a W (VV). It may be referred to as a 'Marion mark 'and is probably the most common marking found in churches. Beginning with religious connotations (and used in church art as well as graffiti) it later became a symbol of good luck, or a mark to ward off ill fortune. Be wary however: John Phillips, our local expert, warns me that many of the marks attributed to religious protection are, in fact, masons marks. What I have selected to write about above barely touches on the complicated history of medieval graffiti - there is so much more. From ship and boat marks, heraldic marks, merchants marks, to fish and puffins all beautifully described and explored in Mathew Champion's book ''Medieval Graffiti - The Lost Voices of England's Churches" which I used as my main source. Read the book - I'm sure you will be intrigued. If nothing else go and look for some of the masons' marks in Beverley Minster, but before you go read John Phillips' article in U3a, and if possible look at 'Of a Faire Uniforme Making' which contains all the masons' marks in the Minster.

APPENDIX 3

FROM SHEEP'S WOOL TO CLOTH

Farmers reared and sheared the sheep. The packmen or laniers took the fleeces to market.

PROCESSING TO CLOTH

1. **Sorting** - separated into groups based on coarseness. Outer fibres were longer, thicker and coarser and were spun to make worsted yarn. Inner layers were softer and were spun to make woollen yarn.

2. **Cleansing** – washed in soap and water.

3. **Beating** - wool was hung on wooden slats to dry and then beaten with sticks (usually of willow). This separated tangles and removed foreign matter.

4 **Dyeing** - sometimes performed at this stage and called 'dyed in the wool' or preliminary dyeing.

5. **Greasing** - with butter or olive oil - protected the wool during the processing and made easier to handle.

6. **Carding or Combing** - to separate and straighten the fibres. Combing with two wooden combs or carding using flat wooden boards and hooks. Bowing was also used - when wool was hung from a bow and string and the string hit with a mallet to make it vibrate and separate the wool.

7. **Spinning** - drop spindles and later spinning wheels.

8. **Weaving -** into a rough cloth (wefts and warps).

9. **Fulling or Walking** - took the grease out of the cloth and made it tighter and thicker.

10. **Drying on -** tenter frames and hooks.

11. **Shearing -** removed the fuzzy surface layer.

12. **Napping or teaseling -** raised the nap of the fabric and gave a soft smooth finish. Used head of a plant called teasel*(dipsacus)*.

13. **Dyeing**

14. **Pressing**

APPENDIX 4

YELLOW BOOTS

I have always loved Van Gogh's paintings of "The Two Shoes". On the inside front cover of the original guide to The Trail is a plaque depicting two yellow boots. I really thought these were Van Gogh's. When I enlarged the picture, it was quite clear that this was incorrect. The boots were the same as the ones shown on page 12 of the guide, where the Cordwainers installation is a pattern for the aforementioned boot. I found a similar boot in the Medieval Museum display at Humber Museums, but where it came from I do not know. Berna Moody told me that the boots on the cover were the original symbol for The Town Trail - rather I suppose in the way of "These boots are made for walking". I rather liked that idea, even though it may not be true. Anyway, I painted my own interpretation of Van Gogh's Two Shoes and call it "Yellow Boots". We decided to use it on the front cover and again after Berna's Epilogue, as a symbol of the end of the walk.

SOURCES

1.THE BUTCHERS
1.The History of the Butcher: www.turnerandgeorge.co.uk
2.Butchery's long History: www.history.com [video]
3.Medieval Meat : www.medieval-life-and-times/medieval-food/medieval -meathtm

2.THE WALKERS and FULLERS
1.WorstJobs in the Middle Ages/06/The Fuller: youtube.com/watch?v=Vb0V5NSgAo0
2. allthats interesting.com/awful-jobs/9
3.urbo.com/content/worst-jobs-from-british-history-that-will-make -you-appreciate -yours
4 https:middle-ages-turkey.weeby.com/worst-jobs-in--middle-ages.html

3.THE CORDWAINER
1 susannamnewstead.co.uk/2018/04/01/mediaeval-trades-the-cordwainer
2. Making new shoes from new leather: en Wikipedia.org/wiki/Cordwainer
3 Cordwainers.org/about-us The Worshipful Company of Cordwainers
4 Making Medieval Turnshoes: www.youtube.com/watch?v=GfdybrK8ZVw

4.THE SPINNERS
1.Katrin Kania in Was Medieval Spinning a Woman's Work?: the freelancehistorywriter.com/
   tag/womens-history-3/ 2015/10/23
2. Medieval Spinning: aprilmundy.wordpress.com/tag/medieval-spinning
3 A woman's work was never done: plymagazine.com/2020/07/spinning-in-medieval-art

5.THE DYERS
1. Rosalie's Medieval Woman:rosaliegilbert.com/dyes and colours.html
2. Jenny Balfour-Paul in 'Indigo' British Museum Press 1998
3. Viking Age Dyes: Evidence and Methods:sites.google.com/site/zoemcdonell/naturaldyeing.

6.THE CARTMEN
1.Beverley Minster.org.uk/ top-10-things-to-see
2.beverley.org.uk/product/explorers-guide-to-beverley-minster: by Pamela Hopkins, Hallgarth
   Publishing
3.The Misericords of Beverley Minster D.Phil. Thesis by Malcolm Haydn Jones: core.ac,uk/
   download/pdf/29816745.pdf

7.THE GLOVEMAKERS
1. en Wikipedia.org/wiki/glove
2 Gloves in Medieval and Renaissance Culture: www.lardatter.com
3 Mike Redwood:www.mikeredwood.com/all-about-gloves/

8.THE JERKIN MAKERS
1. A leather jerkin well examined : www.museum of london.org,uk/discover/leather- jerkin-
   well-examined
2. www.en Wikipedia.org/wiki/Jerkin
3.fashionhistory.fitnyc.edu/jerkin

9.THE MINSTRELS
1. beverleyminster.org.uk/visit-us-2/misericords
2. gladysstrickland.com/medieval-minstrel-carvings-in-beverley-minster
3. yorkshireguides.com/beverley (click St Marys)
4. The Origin of the Town Waits, and the myth of the watchmen turned musician by Richard
   Rastall:townwaits.org.uk/essays/waitsorigin.pdf/(deadlink)
5.Walter L. Woodfill in Musicians in English Society from Elizabeth to Charles 1: Princeton
   University Press, Princton NJ,1953

10. THE ARMOURERS
1. www. en wikipedia.org/wiki/ Plate_armour
2. www. en wikipedia.org/wiki/List_of_medieval_armour_ components
3. warhistoryonline.com/medieval/7-types-of -armour.html
4. www,en wikipeda,org/wiki/Chain_mail
5. www.historyextra.com/peroid//medieval/how-did-knights-in-armour-go-to-the-toilet
6. How to put on plate armour: Youtube.com/watch?v=V8-eeJUco5M

11. THE TILERS and BRICKLAYERS
1. Rise and Decline of the Guilds:Tim Hoffman:tylersandbricklayers.co.uk/images/stories/ guilds.pdf [fantastic summary!]
2. susannamnewstead.co.uk/2018/05/25/ medieval-tradesmen-the-tiler
3. Women in Medieval Guilds: Lady MagdaleneSaunders www.Lothene.org/feudalist/ newsletter/guilds.htlm
4. Guild: en Wikipedia.org/wiki/Guild

12. THE LORIMERS and THE FARRIERS
1. eastridingmuseums.co.uk/EasySiteWeb/EasySite/StyleData/culture/downloads/museums/past-exhibits/skidby-mill/tools-of-the-trade.pdf
2. All Things Mediaeval : An Encylopedia of the Medieval World:Ruth A Johnson 2011, Google books
3. Craftsmen and Industry in late medieval time in York :thesis by H.C.Swanson https://core. ac.uk/download/pdf/42604787.pdf
4. Blacksmith:en Wikipedia.org/wiki/ Blacksmith
5. oldfieldforge.co.uk/history-of-blacksmithing/
6. medievalbritain.com/type/medieval-life/occupations/medieval-blacksmith

13 and 33. THE WINDMILLERS and THE WATER MILLERS
1. East Riding Water-mills : KJ Allison: East Yorkshire Local History Society, 1970
2. East Yorkshire Windmills: Roy Gregory: Charles Skilton Publishing,1985

THE BAKERS
1. hkcarms,tripod,com/oc3.html : Baker, Barrister and Bookbinder
2. www. thefinertimes.com middle ages (scroll to bakers)
3. Https://medievalbritain.com/type/medieval-life/occupations/medieval-baker

15. THE GOLDSMITHS
1. What is Goldsmithing:https:// www.visual-arts-cork.com>goldsmithing
2. A brief history of the Minster: beverleyminster.org.uk
3. Goldsmith:en.wikipedia,org/wiki/Goldsmith

16. THE HATTERS
1. Headware of the Middle Ages : www. encylopedia.com
2. Early History of Felt making in London by Harry Duckwith: www.feltmakers.co.uk/wp-content/uploads/2017/08/Feltmakers-Research-Paper-Final-version-pdf
3. thedecavershamhousehold.wordpress.com/2015/02/15/historical-mens-headwear
4. The jester: simple Wikipedia.org/wiki/Jester
5. socialstudies,org/system/files/publications/articles/se_77021364,pdf Role of Guilds in Business in Middle ages
6. Excerpt from The Articles of the Heaumers and the Hatters :A Source Book of London History from Earliest Times to 1800 ed P Meadows London B Belland Sons Ltd,1914 pp44

17.THE BOWYERS and the FLETCHERS

1. Longbow : A Social and Military History: Robert Hardy: Lyons Press,1993
2 Beverley Town Records: East Riding Archives: eastriding.gov.uk/leisure/archives-family-and-local-history
3 www.historyforkids.net/medieval-arrows.htlm
4 Arrows : en.wikipedia.org/wiki/ Arrow
5 https:// www.archerylibrary.com>books> Toxophilus

18.THE TAILORS

1. thoughtco.com :medieval- underwear-1788621 [by Melissa Small]
2. edition.cnn.com/2009/LIVING/homestyle/10/27/mf.men.underwear.history/
3. BBC History Magazine Aug 2012 Medieval Underwear: historyextra.com/period/medieval/medieval-underwear-bras-pants-and-lingerie-in-the-middle-ages/

19.THE APOTHECARIES

1. William Bulleyn in The Apothecary in England from the 13thC to Close of the 16thC: by CTS
2. Traditional Treatments in the Medieval Era: www.bbc.co.ukbitesize:guides/zwkm97h/revision/1
3   when-wise-women-were-witches:liviecampbell.medium.com
4   The Night with the Lion:abdn,ac,uk/sll/disciplines/English/lion/knight26.shtml

20.THE BARBER SURGEONS

1.brainblogger.com/2011/05/06/from-haircuts-to-hangnails-the-barber-surgeon
2. www.history.com/news/why-are-barbers-poles-red-white-and-blue
3. Barber Surgeon: en.wikipedia/wiki/Barber_Surgeon
4. https://books.google.co.uk/edition/At-the- sign-of -the barbers-pole/ The Goat without a Beard Fable by John Gay 1727:

21.THE MERCHANTS and CRAFTSMENS GUILDS   [not proofed]

1.www.medieval-life- and -times.info/medieval-life/medieval-merchant.htm
2.Merchant: en. wikipedia.org/wiki/Merchant
3.thefinertimes.com/merchants-in-the-middle-ages
4 ducksters.com/history/middle_ages_guilds.php

22.THE FISHTRADERS and SHIPMEN

1.earlychurchhistory.org/commerce/ancient-fishmongers
2.The Fishmonger: en.wikipedia.org/wiki/ Fishmonger
3 The History of the Fishmongers Company: fishmongers.org/our-history

23.THE PRINTERS

1.The Misericords of Beverley Minster: PhD Thesis. Malcolm Haydn Jones : pearl.plymouth.ac.uk/handle/10026.1/628
2.Thoughtco.com/history-of -printing-and- printing-process-1992329
3.christstreasures.blogspot.com/2018/03/christs-colleges-historic-wallpaper.html
4.Personal communication: Berna Moody

24.THE STONE MASONS – Further reading:

1. 'Of a Fair Uniforme Making' The building of Beverley Minster 1188-1736 by John Phillips. beverleyminster.org.uk/product/of-a-fair-uniforme-making-by-john-phillips/
2. The Medieval Stonemason and Gothic Cathedrals (Society of Architectural Historians) by Deyem Akande:sah.org/publications-and-research/sah-blog/sah-blog/2017/07/18/medieval-masons-and-gothic-cathedrals/
3. The Medieval Stonemason by Carol Davidson Cragoe (assistant architectural editor of the Victorian County History) bbc.co.uk history/british/middle_ages/architecture_medmason_01.shtml

25. THE BREWERS
1. John Barleycorn:en.wikipedia.org/wiki/John_Barleycorn
2 The Story Behind the Song:John Barleycorn by Traffic: https://musicaficionado.blog/2016/02/15/john-barleycorn-by-traffic
3 John Barleycorn by Stevie Winwood,acoustic :youtube.co/watch?v=t8878chOvfl

26. THE CARPENTERS
1 Builders and Decorators:' Medieval Craftsmen in Wales', Nicola Coldstream, Cadw, Welsh Assembly Government, 2008 [Lovely little book]
2 The Medieval Woodworkers Toolbox : thomasguild.blogspot.com/2011/01/ medieval-woodworkers-toolboxhtml

27. THE SADDLERS
1. Medieval Saddles: en.wikipedia.org/wiki/Saddle
2. Horses in the Middle Ages: en.wikipedia.org/wiki/Horses-in-the-Middle-Ages
3. Medieval Saddle factory: http//medieval;-saddle- factory.de
4. How does a modern saddle compare to a Medieval Saddle youtube.com/watch?v=siFbuKaxNzo

28. THE WEAVERS
1. British History Online: british-history.ac.uk/vch/yorks/east/vol6
2 Pamela Hopkins in The History of Beverley:Blackthorn Press, 2nd Ed 2011
3 Cabbages and Kings :A History of Saturday Market,Beverley: Barbara English et al Beverley and District Civic Society,2014
4 www.midtudormanor.wordpresscom/making-cloth
5 Thought.com/manufaturing-cloth-from-wool-1788611 (great article}

29. THE ROPE MAKERS – further reading
1. A condensed history of rope making: HW Dickinson : core.tdar.org/document/421163/a-condensed-history-of -ropemaking
2. The Story of Rope Making – The Ropewalk Barton on Humber: www.ropewalkco,uk (choose museum)
3 The Batsford Companion to Local History : Stephen Friar: Batsford Ltd pub:1998

30. THE CREELER
1. The Beverley Beck Heritage Walk: heritage-now.weebly.com/uploads/3/0/2/1/30217551/Beverley.pdf

31. THE WILDFOWLERS
1. Man and Wildfowl: Janet Kear: publishers: T and AD Poyser:1990
2. Watertown: eastridingmuseums.co.uk/EasySiteWeb/EasySite/StyleData/culture/downloads/museums/past-exhibitions/beverley-guildhall/watertown.pdf
3. Medievalists. net/2016/05/swan-you-say-medieval-feasting
4. William Strickland:wasleys.org.uk/eleanor/churches/england/yorkshire/east_ riding/east_one/Boynton/index.htlm

32. THE POTTERS
1.differencebetween.net/object/difference-between-pottery-and-ceramics
2. the potterywheel.com /what-is-the-difference-between-pottery and -ceramics
3. Humber Archaeology Partnership : Medieval pottery -manufactured in Beverley Information sheet 5 (supplied by Berna Moody)

33. THE WATER MILLERS and 13. THE WINDMILLERS
1. East Riding Watermills : KJ Allison: East Yorkshire Local History Society, 1970
2. East Yorkshire Wind Mills: Roy Gregory: Charles Skilton Publishing,1985

34.THE TANNERS

1. Tanning in the Town: www. eastridingmuseums.co.uk
2. Kim Renfield: Unusual Historicals: Odd Jobs-A Medieval Dirty Job: http://unusualhistoricals. blogspot.com/ 2016/11/odd-jobs-tanning-medieval- dirty-job.html

35.THE COOPER

1.Cooper: en.wikipedia.org/wiki/Cooper
2.allisondreid.com/tag/medieval-cooper
3 George Smithwick:Traditional Cooper: youtube.com/watch?v=GE7QA1chUzw

36.THE SCRIVENERS

1. Scribes and Illuminators(Medieval Craftsmen) by Christopher De Hamel. British Museum Press, 2009
2. The Scriveners Tale by Adam Pankhurst. the guardian.com/uk/2004/jul/20/ highereducation. books
3 Itinerant Scrivener: Medieval Free Company: you tube.com/watch?v=2XBMSXTgo10

37.THE LOCKSMITHS

1. Love laughs at Locksmiths: www.proverbhunter.com
2 www.creativelygraceful.blogspot .com/2017/02/love-laughs-at- locksmiths.htlm
3. Workingtheflame.com/history-of-locksmithing
4. historicallocks.com/en/site/h/padlocks/the-history-of-padlocks/swedish-middle-ages -1050-1520/

38.THE CHANDLER/CANDLEMAKERS

1. Chandlery: the-history-girls-blogspot.com/2018/01/trade—in-the-17th-century-tallow-chandler.htlm
2 History of the Wax Chandler: en.wikipedia.org/wiki/Worshipful_ Company_ of_ Wax_ Chandlers
3. Our History-Tallow Chandlers:www.tallowchandlers.org/about-us/our-history/historical-narratives/need-to-know-facts-about-the-history-of-the-tallow-chandlers
4. The work of the Chandler in Medieval Times:worldhistory.us/medieval-history/the -occupation- of-chandler- in -the -medieval-ages.php

39.THE FISHMONGERS

1.Fishing in Medieval Times: www.cliffehistory.co.uk/fishing.html
2.medievalists.net/2020/11/medieval- fishing
3 https://siglindesarts.wordpress.com>medieval-fishing

40.THE COOKS

1.Medieval cuisine: en wkipedia.org/wiki/Medieval_cuisine
2 Joy V Spicer Mediaeval Foods :www.joyvspicer.com/joy-blog/2018/10/16/medieval-food

41. MEDIEVAL GRAFFITI

1.Medieval Graffiti Mathew Champion,Ebury Press,2015
2.historicengland.org.uk/whats -new/features/discovering -witch- marks/
3.nationaltrust.co.uk/features/witch-marks-these-marks
4.devonhistoricgraffiti.org.uk/v-v-symbol-and -other-related -letters
5. u3asites.org.uk/files/b/beverley/docs/8-beverleyminstertour.pdf
6 Marks of the Witch:Britains ritual protection symbols Thesis by David Clarke available at www.shura.shu.ac.uk/26362
7 Of a Faire Uniforme Making- The Building History of Beverley Minster 1188-1736 : John Phillips ,Blackthorne Press,2016 [available at the Minster Bookshop]

HELP FOR HEALTH: HELPING THE PEOPLE OF EAST YORKSHIRE and NORTH LINCOLNSHIRE

Formerly known as The Humberside Charitable Health Trust, the charity was formed and registered in 2002 under the chairmanship of Roger King. In January of 2011 it was relaunched with a new name - "Help for Heath". The Charity's Mission Statement is:

" Improving the health and wellbeing of people living in East Yorkshire and Northern Lincolnshire".

In seeking to achieve this aim the charity has, over the last two decades, awarded grants totalling £4 million. Help for Health's financial assistance has supported local health related projects both big and small – from supporting major medical research to improving the health and lifestyles of individuals and groups. The charity is controlled by a board of eight trustees (with expertise in business, nursing, administration, accountancy, medicine and the law) under the chairmanship of Dr Andrew Milner. In 2022 Help for Health reaches an important milestone when it celebrates its 20th Anniversary. All profits from this book will be donated to Help for Health as part of this celebration.

Please visit the website at **www.HelpHealth.org.uk** to obtain a more detailed account of the Charity's work, terms of funding and instruction for application.